CHARISMA
Visionary Leadership

Collaborative group power relationship, a form
of imaginary drama where people transform,
act and reflect upon human condition with the
leader as a conductor of the people's vision

Jo Bac

Order this book online at www.trafford.com
or email orders@trafford.com

Most Trafford titles are also available at major online book retailers.

Author Photo by: Grant Triplow

Printed in the United States of America.

ISBN: 978-1-4907-1743-2 (sc)
ISBN: 978-1-4907-1744-9 (e)

Trafford rev. 11/16/2013

 www.trafford.com

North America & international
toll-free: 1 888 232 4444 (USA & Canada)
fax: 812 355 4082

Table of Contents

To my mother

Abstract

The Aim of the Study

This study identifies Barack Obama's charismatic leadership as a visionary leadership model appropriate for the modern era and recognizes a need for further qualitative study. Previous research understood vision as an attribute of the leader, but here it is hypothesized that the vision belongs to the people, the participants of the dramatic interaction called 'charisma'. Obama's charismatic leadership is analysed as dramatic performance, a process of internal and external transformation of all its players. This kind of drama is about changing the nature or condition of the actual world by creating a fiction through the imagination of the followers. This process can become actual and real if followed up by actions. Hence, the manner in which charisma can become actual part of the participants' real life depends on their own way of acting.

The Design of the Study

This study is designed to analyse Obama's speeches and Obama's performance as an exceptionally well developed dramatic process. The drama is a series of actions which leads to the transformation of the nation and creation of the charismatic leadership. The latter is created in the process of the utilisation of drama, which awakened the American Nation's imagination. In addition, the idea of a fictional, imagined and created world may take place only when supported by the actual and real facts. The American Nation as a player, or participant of the political drama, and the leader—Obama, will consider the fiction as an alternative to the real world, in each of these Obama's 'performance'. The American Nation via its imagination gave the reality to it. The role of Obama, the leader, is to find a focus that creates an imperative tension and provides the vehicle for themes to be explored. Moreover, the leader's role is to generate political drama that triggers the emergence of a charismatic relationship. The political leader becomes a tutor, a story teller, whose aim is to create a world where the important questions should be raised.

The state of being real or actual depends on the American Nation and its relation to the fiction created by Obama's drama, to allow people to construct their own unique but united ('the American Dream', 'we can do this'[1]) ways of understanding the world. Obama raised the questions: the American Nation is looking for the answers. The leader's proactivity in this process of charismatic drama creation does not mean he is instructing the nation as to what to do, but rather provides a vehicle for themes to be explored (Jon Scieszka).[2]

The Methodology of the Study

The methodological approach for this study consists of evidence from Obama's performance. In essence, the research relies on two types and sources of data: the theoretical literature and Obama's speeches. The qualitative methodology was based on analysing written and spoken Obama speeches from the drama process point of view. The way of approaching and thinking about the charismatic visionary leadership led this study into the direction of discourse analysis, to be able to approach the charismatic visionary leadership

---

[1]   Obama, B. *Turn the Page Speech*. California Democratic National Convention, April 28, 2007. [Internet]. Available from:<http://obamaspeeches.com>, [Accessed 29 August 2009].

[2]   Taylor, P. (2000) *The drama classroom: action, reflection, transformation*. Routledge, pp.9.

not only from the Obama leadership perspective, but to acquire the holistic, comprehensive view of charisma as a visionary leadership. The aim of this discourse analysis was to expand the previous charisma approaches, which as this paper explains, did not take into consideration the nation as the one which is the co-creator of the leader's vision in the process of the creation of the charismatic leadership.

The Findings of the Study

This study finds that Obama's visionary charismatic leadership is a 'drama process', initiated by the leader—Obama and his use of 'pastoral power' and the drama process. The pastoral power, as well as the drama process, is based on the technology of individualisation/alienation, which awakens different dynamics inside of and between each of the individuals in the American Nation. Furthermore, one of the main tools of the technology of individualisation/alienation is the 'technique of confession'. In this manner, the leader—Obama, (one individual from the American Nation) and the rest of the American Nation, are trying to rediscover and go back to the roots of their traditions and culture (mainly from the view point of the American Dream). Thus, Obama's charismatic visionary leadership is not a 'top to toe' process, or the reverse. His leadership charisma is a process of relationship and transformation of the American Nation based on different dynamics (which have been awakened via the drama process). This takes the form of different ideas, dreams and plans. Created by each of the individuals from the American Nation by their imagination, with the leader as the conductor/shepherd who gives the pretext, the so called story (his personal 'confession'). This initiates relationship—Charisma a visionary leadership; a movement co-created between the leader, here Barack Obama and the American Nation.

1. Objectives

The objectives of this dissertation are to answer the following questions:

1. How does charismatic leadership manifest itself and operate?

2. What explains the success or failure of charismatic movements?

3. Is it possible, to create the charismatic power relationship? If yes, how?

4. What factors account for the ongoing success/effectiveness of this kind of charismatic relation? [Differential treatment, national culture, individual factors etc.]

5. How do the participants/co-creators of the charismatic relationship perceive themselves?

6. Is a political illusionary vision the attitude of the nation of the charismatic power relation with a leader who only conducts and awakens the passions and dreams of a nation, or in a charismatic power relationship the leader need to prove to be able to find answers to critical experiences?

7. Is the charismatic relationship directed by reason, proved and rational visions or by the creation of drama?

2. Background

Charisma—Previous Research

'If there is anyone out there who doubts that America is a
place where anything is possible, who still wonders if the
dream of our founders is alive in our time, who still questions
the power of our democracy, tonight is your answer,'[3]

When a senator from Illinois, Barack Obama has become the first
Afro-American President-Elect of the United States it is not only a
personal victory. As this study is going to investigate, it is the triumph
of drama called charisma. We need to put a question, if there is
any possible way of understanding the phenomenon as charisma.
Is charisma a 'gift' or maybe a 'divine favour'? As the original world
χάρισμα *(kharisma)* derived from Ancient Greek, states.[4] Moreover,
charisma is perceived as interpersonal human qualities which
include exceptionally unusual charm or so called 'magnetic' future
of personality, which is followed by an extraordinary visible aspect of
the person which goes along with their influential convincingness.[5]

---

[3]   Obama, B., *Acceptance speech*, Wednesday 5 November 2008. [Internet].
Available from: <www.guardian.co.uk>, [Accessed 29 August 2009].

[4]   Bligh, M.C., Kohles J. C. (2009) The enduring allure of charisma*:*
How Barack Obama won the historic 2008 presidential election. *The
Leadership Quarterly*, 20 (3) June, pp. 483-492.

[5]   House, R. J., Spangler, W. D., Woycke, J. (1991) Personality and
charisma in the U.S. presidency: A psychological theory of leader
effectiveness. *Administrative science quarterly*, 36, pp. 364-396.

Furthermore, for the first time the term charisma was introduced as a sociological category by Max Weber. According to Weber, charisma is:

> '(. . .) a certain quality of an individual personality, by virtue of which s/he is "set apart" from ordinary people and treated as endowed with supernatural, superhuman, or at least specifically exceptional powers or qualities. These as such are not accessible to the ordinary person, but are regarded as divine in origin or as exemplary, and on the basis of them the individual concerned is treated as a leader.'[6]

In addition, as summarised by Johannes Steyrer there are three social science concepts of charisma:[7] the Leader-centred, (Willner 1984; Conger and Kanungo 1987; Howell and Frost 1989; Puffer 1990; Howell and Higgins 1990; House et al. 1991; Kirkpatrick and Locke 1996; Deluga 1997) in which: charisma depends on the followers' perception of the leader's performance and his/her behaviour. Hence, we need to give meaning to the leader's acts, which will establish him/her as charismatic. (e.g. Conger and Kanungo 1987). The activity of the relation between the leader and his/her followers depends entirely on the leader's actions. Moreover he/she is the one who projects his/her image onto the inactive followers.

Followers-centred; in contrary to the first charisma approach this one entirely depends on a followers' performance, whereas the leader behaves in an inactive or submissive way. Consequently, we need to address the question—What is the reason that makes the followers convey an impression of distinguishing characteristics to the leader? (Downton, 1973; Miyahara 1983; Meindl 1990; Meindl 1992; Mayo et al. 1994). Hence, the activity of the relation between the leader

---

6   Weber, M., In: Eisenstadt SN, editor. *On Charisma and Institution Building.* Chicago: Yale University Press; [1977. re-issued].

7   Steyrer, J. (1998) Charisma and the Archetypes of Leadership. *Organization Studies*, 19 (5), pp. 807-828.

and his/her followers depends entirely on the follower's actions, which leads to the projection of charisma onto the leader if only the focal person demonstrates the validity of his/hers statements to critical situations. Consequently, the Leader-centred approach as well as the Followers-centred one, narrows the relationship between the leader and his/her followers to only one active side interaction.

The last, introduced to the sociology concept of charisma came into existence as an Interdependency-oriented; Beyond what has been stated, this is the first idea of charisma which acknowledges the active interaction between both sides (the leader and his/hers followers). Moreover, during the critical experiences, the extraordinary leader enters into a relationship with the followers, who are in a state of a mental or emotional strain. Thus, charisma needs to be analysed in a correlative way, instead of as it was stated in previous concepts, in a linear manner—either 'top to toe', the leader centred approach; or, in reverse, the followers-centred one. (Schweitzer 1984; Lindholm 1990; Pauchant 1991; Shamir et al. 1993; House and Shamir 1993)

In addition to what has been said already, it would be essential to mention Charles Lindholm's concept of charisma:

> 'Charisma is, above all, a relationship, a mutual mingling of the inner selves and leader and follower. Therefore, it follows that if the charismatic is able to compel, the follower has a matching capacity for being compelled, and we need to consider what makes up the personality configuration of the follower, and well as that of the leader, if we are to understand charisma.'[8]

As we may notice, the core of the Lindholm's approach to the concept as charisma leads us to the idea of 'relationship'. Thus, the

---

[8]   Lindholm, C. (2002) *Charisma*. [Internet] Available from: <http://www.bu.edu/uni/faculty/profiles/charisma.pdf>, [Accessed 29 August 2009].

interpersonal qualities of the leader become essential, but not crucial, for the interchange between the leader and his/her followers as charisma.

This study will examine the phenomenon of Obama's charismatic leadership by developing the interdependency-orientated theory and that of Lindholm, in order to more fully understand the idea of visionary leadership. This in all of the above approaches is understood as a vision of the leader. In this study however, the understanding of charisma is as the relationship where the vision is co-created by the participants with the leader as a conductor.

3. The New Theory
of Charismatic Leadership

'Collaborative group power relationship, a form of imaginary drama where people transform, act and reflect upon human condition with the leader as a conductor of the people's vision.'[9]

There is a considerable confusion as to the proper function of politics as well as theatre. In our contemporary world, theatre as well as politics appears incapable of dealing with the significant aspects of life. Technology has created a new vision of the world. Television, radio, and the internet have established new standards of immediacy and actuality. As a result, politics and theatre has been relegated to entertainment. Furthermore, the political stage as well as the theatrical one has gone through several transformations. The most important transformation is the introduction of mass media in order to make both politics and theatre capable of handling twenty first century issues. The world creates two stages, a political and a theatrical. Two political theatres, but which one is the creator of the real world and which one of the illusion?

3.1. Epic Theatre and the Alienation Effect

'Since all political systems require at least some mythology (or 'golden lies') for their functioning, the patterns and

---

9   Ibid., (The New Theory of Charisma)

dynamics of political illusion are by no means insignificant subjects for study'[10]

We may conclude that both of those stages bring into being 'illusion' or 'so called fiction'. The erroneous perception of reality was brought into being by the use of different tools. Is there any difference between those tools which both, theatre and politics, use in their creation of a fictional appearance and deceptive impression of reality? Let us look closer at the mechanics and tools used by theatre in theatrical performance creation to give a better idea of those used on the political stage.

The idea of fictional, possible worlds as an alternative to the actual world derives from two kinds of dramatic fiction: first, that which is true according to the real world—possible according to necessity and second, that which is true according to possibility—possible as an alternative to the actual world. In theatre, this issue becomes Stanislavsky and his idea of performance and theatre, versus Brecht and his idea of the epic theatre. But if those two different kinds of dramas will be merged, the third drama, charisma, may appear.

> 'In reaching the spectators, theatre can adopt to main channels; the intellect (mainly addressed by the Brecht's alienation effect) or the emotions (Aristotle's catharsis). Any combination of these two is possible'[11]

The aim of the dramatic theatre is to create the effect of reflection and consideration, which in the dramatic performance is brought into being by ontological topics.

> 'The dramatic theatre's spectator says: Yes, I have felt like that too—Just like me—It's only natural—It'll never

---

[10] Weissberg, R. (1975) Political Efficacy and Political. *The Journal of Politics,* 37 (2) May, p.469-487.

[11] Carr, B. (1996) *Morals and society in Asian Society.* Routledge, pp.119.

> change—The sufferings of this man appal me, because
> they are inescapable—That's great art; it all seems the most
> obvious thing in the world—I weep when they weep, I
> laugh when they laugh' (B. Brecht)[12]

The idea of the epic theatre performs on the contrary to the dramatic one. Thus, its aim is to raise the issues of the social and political values. Moreover, the epic stage was intended to describe life in its realistic and actual frames. Accordingly, the main importance became the reduction of the distance between the stage and the audience of the epic theatre. As noticed by Kaja Silverman 'The stage is still elevated. But it no longer rises from an unfathomable depth: it has become a public platform.'[13] Consequently, the so-called 'forth wall' understood as an imagined wall which exists between the audience and the ones who perform on a stage, disappeared.[14]

> 'The epic theatre's spectator says: I'd never have thought
> of it—That's not the way—That's extraordinary, hardly
> believable—It's got to stop—The sufferings of that man
> appal me, because they are unnecessary—That's great art;
> nothing obvious in it—I laugh when they weep, I weep
> when they laugh.' (B. Brecht)[15]

The alienation effect is the main tool of the epic theatre. Brecht wrote, '(. . .) stripping the event of its self-evident, familiar, obvious quality and creating a sense of astonishment and curiosity about them.'[16] In terms of charismatic leadership there is the clash between,

---

[12] Brecht, B., Willett, J. (1964) *Brecht on theatre: the development of an aesthetic.* Hill and Wang, pp.71.

[13] Silverman, K. (1984) The *Subject of Semiotics.* New York: Oxford University Press.

[14] Stevenson, K. (1995) *The fourth wall and the third space.* Centre for Playback Theatre.

[15] Ibid., pp.71.

[16] Thomson, P., Sacks, G. (2006) *The Cambridge companion to Brecht.* Cambridge University Press, pp.191.

for example, the idea of American Dream or 'we can do this' and the Obama's statements about reforms of healthcare and the educational system, during the Presidential Campaign in United States.[17] The aim is to 'push the viewer to establish some distance in his relation to reality'. Thus, for example the American Nation faced the typical effect of alienation, which acts in such a manner that each individual is prevented from feeling his way into the one who gave the performance—Obama, the leader. Furthermore, the alienation effect woke up the American Nation's emotions and imagination, which does not have to be identical with that as presented by Obama. This way of acting and performing is the leading and conducting of the participant of the performance against the away how exactly the actor or the leader is feeling, dreaming or imagining. Moreover, this allows the participants to create their own unique way of interpreting the events.

In theory the alienation effect seems to be a successful one, but unfortunately when facing the practice even Brecht admitted that it fell short of his expectations.[18] In addition, the actors in epic theatre were still emotional linked as the performer and the part he/she was stepping into to the Aristotelian way of acting. Thus, it was impossible for the performer not to 'attach' to their role. Hence, it would be very difficult even for the theatrical participants to eliminate all kinds of emotional experience.[19]

Nevertheless, another creator of the epic theatre, Foreman, put to practical use the alienation effect, but only to express spiritual,

---

[17] Obama, B., *Turn the Page Speech*, California Democratic National Convention, April 28, 2007. [Internet] Available from: <http://obamaspeeches.com/>, [Accessed 29 August 2009].

[18] McTeague, J. H. (1994) *Playwrights and Acting: Acting Methodologies for Brecht, Ionesco, Pinter, and Shepard.* Westport: Greenwood Press, pp.24-25.

[19] Gassner, J. (1954) Dramatic and Detachment: A View of Brecht's Style of Theatre. *The Theatre in Our Times: A Survey of the Men, Materials and Movements in the Modern Theatre.* New York: Crown Publishers, pp.82-96.

ontological (ontology—the science of being)[20] avoiding the social and political, issues. Moreover, Foreman was taking under consideration only those concerns, which lead to the ontology of consciousness and thought. Thus, Foreman's aim was to understand and express the ways to shape the consciousness during the created performance. 'Empirical evidence suggests that transcendental consciousness is a field that links all individuals (Travis 1989)'.[21]

> 'The performer initially creates *rasa*—transcendental self-transcendental consciousness—as the basis of the mind and encompassing not only, by definition the emotions, but all levels of the expressed mind, i.e. ego, emotions, intellect, mind, desire and senses. This state of *rasa* is communicated to the spectators on all those levels of the mind.'[22]

The participants of the Foreman's theatre were lead to reflect on the issue of the performance in their own individual way. Performance was supposed to be understood without 'wandering and looking' for the director's or creator's hidden intentions. Moreover, this kind of technique woke the audience up to the ability of achieving their own understanding of the play. Foreman's aim is to keep the audience away from enjoying the old, habitual understanding of performed actions. Analysing Obama's performance, we may assume that he was able to use this same technique by expressing the political issues together with metaphorical sentences as in 'turn the page', 'we can make it or 'my father had a dream', which are not commonly use in political or high importance speeches or performances. Hence, in Foreman's theatre the spectators do not focus on the essence of the created actions, on the things itself, but are forced to look for their own meaning, and to find the answers between the words and/or

---

20   Bunge, M.A. (1977) *Ontology.* Volume 1, Springer.
21   Ibid., pp.122.
22   Ibid., pp.122.

operating part of the performance.[23] In addition, we may notice that if Obama applied this kind of method in his speeches, the importance of the political and economical issues was taken over the American Nation without justification. Moreover, each individual could fulfils Obama's words with their own interpretation. "If everything depends on my interpretation, who can guarantee that I interpret right?"[24]

> 'I want to refocus the attention of the spectator on the intervals, gaps, relations and rhythms which saturate the objects (acts and physical props) which are the 'givens' of any particular play. In doing this, I believe the spectator is made available (as I am, hopefully, when writing) to those most desirable energies which secretly connect him (through a kind of resonance) with the foundation of his being.'[25]

Foreman was the one who rejected the idea of illusion and emotional engagement in his performances, denying the traditional Aristotelian theatre, as did Brecht. Moreover, Foreman noticed that the traditional theatre blocks the audiences' subjective understanding of the performed issues.[26] However, Foreman was the one who used the elements of ontology in his theatre. In addition, Foreman noticed the relation between the ontological concerns of his play with the Brecht's alienation effect. Nevertheless, he narrowed the issues of being only to the ontology of consciousness. Consequently, what if the dramatic

---

[23] Kiwonlee, B.A. (2001) *The Dynamics of Richard Foreman's Theatre:* Text and performance [Internet]. Available from: <http://etd. lib.ttu.edu/theses/available/etd-09262008-31295017969758/ unrestricted/31295017969758.pdf>, [Accessed 29 August 2009].

[24] Steele, R., Swinney S.V. (1982) Freud *and Jung, conflict of interpretation.* Law Book Co of Australasia, pp.361.

[25] Davy, K. (1978) Richard Foreman's Ontological-Hysteric Theatre: The Influence of Gertrude Stein. *Twentieth Century Literature*, 24 (1) Spring, pp.108-126.

[26] Davy, K. (1981) Richard Foreman and the Ontological-Hysteric Theatre. *Issue 2 of Theatre and dramatic studies.* UMI Research Press.

performance merged not only the elements from Brecht's theatre (the alienation effect) and the ontology of consciousness? What if the performance brings back the issues of everyday life? What if the social and political concerns appear along with the ontological?

3.2 Dramatic Theatre and its 'Praxis' ('to do')

What fulfils the idea of epic theatre in terms of charismatic leadership is drama praxis, the interplay between people their imagination and passions. The audience in both terms, as a nation or theatre participants, are the co-creators of the drama praxis with a leader-conductor, whose role is to lead in the process as charisma. A political leader conducts the nation, to be able to manipulate itself to wake up its imagination, passions and emotions. Passion is the 'heightened state which can arouse strong and emotive responses'.[27] The passions are directed to the created, fictional world, where the nation wants to find itself. It is the process of stepping into imagined roles and situations.

Furthermore, the leaders' role is to select a material, a story or a pre-text which will lead and raise a focus on cultural aspects of the nation. But in terms of charisma, we are taking into consideration the process, the relationship of its co-players which is so rare in any kind of leadership, for a very simple reason. It is possible to create a drama, power relation which will be believable but meaningless, in which the moments of co-creation, power relation will be convincing but not knit into a coherent meaningful structure—structure of significance and mundane, fictional and real.

> 'Certain circumstances may be changed; milieus are transformed; but man does not change. History is valid for the milieu; but not for man. The milieu is so essentially unimportant, is understood just as the occasion for things.

---

[27] Ibid., pp.2.

A variable quantity, and essentially inhuman, it really exists without man. It confronts him as a closed unity. And he is forever unchanged, a fixed quantity. To regard man as a variable which, moreover, controls the milieu, to conceive of the liquidation of the milieu in relationships between men—these notions spring from a new mode of thought, historical thought.'[28]

The significance (significant contemporary social issues) and its co-relation with the mundane is the factor which separates charismatic effect of power relation, from the general one.

The question is, how to reach this significant/mundane effect, which will lead to the effect as charismatic relationship? How can such a relation be created so that its historical character and actual, present is revealed? The relationship as charismatic can be reached or achieved only when the leader/director comprehends the idea, that though the believability (psychological authenticity) a necessary condition for a successful leader/director performance but not the charismatic drama with a nation-cooperation, creation. Control of the significance of the power/knowledge relationship between free subjects—nation and leader—'human instruments' by which the power can be exercised is the key to charismatic drama creation.

3.3 Power/Knowledge Relationship

In order to understand the significance of the power/knowledge charismatic relation it is necessary to clarify the phenomena of power and knowledge. Power is a central concern of political science. The first idea of power, as a common ability to act, is engaged by people in their relations with others. Weber understands by power: the chance of a man, or a number of men "to realize their own will in

---

[28] Martin, C., Bial, H. (2000) *Brecht Sourcebook*. Routledge, pp.18.

communal action, even against the resistance of others."[29] Such a definition as a common capacity implies an unequal relationship between those who employ power for their own intention or aim and those who are subject to its effects.

> 'At bottom, despite the difference in epochs and objectives, the representation of power has remained under the spell of monarchy. In political thought and analysis we still have not cut off the head of the king'[30]

At the core of the previous concepts of power, Locke's and Hobbes definitions of power is the idea, which focuses on the attributes of the individual. Power as understood by Hobbes or Lock relates to individual attributes and properties; 'Power of a man'.[31] 'We need to cut off the King's head'[32]– Here Foucault managed to transform the idea of power. Power is not acquired is employed and exercised. Power manifests itself through action upon others, which works through people rather then only on them. Power is a relation, a 'structure of actions'.[33]

> 'The exercise of power is not simply a relationship between agents/partners etc, individual or collective; it's the way in which certain actions modify others'[34]

Even if this is possible, to describe one person as having and exercising power over the other, that power depends upon other

---

[29] Chinoy, E. (1967) *Society: an introduction to sociology.* Random House, pp.323.

[30] Gutting, G. (1944) *The Cambridge companion to Foucault.* Cambridge University Press, pp.99.

[31] Raphael, D.D. (2004) *Hobbes: morals and politics.* Routledge, pp.47.

[32] Clifford, M. (2001) *Political genealogy after Foucault: savage identities.* Routledge, pp.15.

[33] Hindess, B. (1996) *Discourses of Power: from Hobbes to Foucault.* Wiley-Blackwell, pp.141.

[34] Ibid., pp.244.

persons or groups acting in concert with what the first person does. Foucault does not conceive of such a relationship as being imposed from the top, down 'the support which force relations find in one another thus forming a chain or system. (. . .) Power (. . .) is the name that one attributes to a complex strategic situation in a particular society'.[35]

The significance of power relation depends on the knowledge of the national and its social relations, which require meanings and frameworks (a cultural arrangement).

> 'The exercise of power itself creates and causes to emerge new objects of knowledge and accumulates new bodies of information (. . .) the exercise of power perpetually creates knowledge and, conversely, knowledge constantly induces effects of power (. . .). It is not possible for power to be exercised with—out knowledge, it is impossible for knowledge not to engender power.' (M. Foucault).[36]

The power/knowledge relationship is based on methods which lead the leader to the knowledge of the nation, via mechanisms of observation and ways of encoding. The knowledge of the individual which has been described and knowledge about may be translated to the leader/director 'as an analysable, describable subject (Burrell)'[37], which can be valuated and considered or described as similar, equal, or analogous with others.

The charismatic drama creation requires a degree of understanding of nation forces, its reactions, its strengths and weaknesses.' The

---

[35] During, S. (2004) *Foucault and Literature: Towards a Genealogy of Writing*. Routledge.

[36] Rasche, A. (2007) *The Paradoxical Foundation of Strategic Management*. Springer, pp.131.

[37] Salaman, G., Storey, J., Billsberry J. (2005) *Strategic human resource management: theory and practice*. SAGE, pp.73.

government of souls and lives that is the entire theme of pastoral power thought'[38] Foucault presents the technology of individualisation with the technique of confession as the most effective power exercise, which makes knowledge of the individual available. Furthermore, this knowledge can be used by the leader and/or director and leads to the charisma, the significant relationship which requires this exceptional type of knowledge of the nation, of their needs and actions—the knowledge of their 'soul'. The pastoral power used the metaphor of 'the shepherd and the flock'. The shepherd, the leader in politics, the director in theatre, exercises pastoral power over the nation, via a more intimate and continuous relationship, which locates individuals in their cultural and traditional place.

> 'Culture as a historically specific set of institutionally embedded relations of government in which the forms of thought and conduct of extended populations are targeted for transformation—in part via the extension through the social body of the forms, techniques, and regimens of aesthetic and intellectual culture. (M. Foucault)'[39]

It is crucial for this paper to go further, to include the interpretation of the Foucault concept of pastoral power and its tools, which leads to the technology of individualisation. As noted before, a leader is one who needs to acquire the knowledge of the people's 'soul'. Thus, he/she needs to understand the nation, the people he leads as a good 'shepherd', and who gains an understanding of his/her 'flock'. Essentially, the technique of confession and observation, should lead to such a comprehension, but only in theory. To bring the Foucault's pastoral power 'alive' and to give to it actual and practical frame, there is the need to include one more technique. The fulfilment of

---

[38] Foucault, M., Burchell, G., Gordon, C., Miller, P. (1991) *The Foucault effect: studies in governmentality: with two lectures by and an interview with Michel Foucault.* University of Chicago Press, pp.87.

[39] McGuigan, J. (1996) *Culture and the public sphere.* Taylor & Francis, pp.14.

his pastoral theory has its deep roots in the technology of alienation, represented by the epic theatre and employed often in Brecht's or Foreman's performances. And as this paper will explain, the alienation effect in a leader/nation relationship leads to the charismatic visionary leadership with the vision co-created by the nation.

3.4 Cultural Purification

The major significance in the area of a charismatic relationship is the theory of the cultural purification. Its three basic elements: rediscovering ('the rediscovery of an ethnic past, and especially of a golden age that can act as an inspiration for contemporary problems and needs' of the nation), validation ('determining what is and what is not distinctive and what therefore can be deemed 'truly ours (of the nation)' and re appropriation ('the people [nation] need to be encouraged to take possession of their authentic vernacular heritage').[40] Those factors, in probability, will lead to a creation of the unified actions of individuals who have shared these same cultural patterns in the past, these—same values.

> 'Certain bodies, certain gestures, certain discourses, certain desires come to be constituted as individuals. The individual (. . .) is I believe one of [power's] prime effects' (M. Foucault)[41]

These are the beliefs of the entire nation, which during the charismatic drama creation are awakened and rediscovered. Moreover,

---

[40] Smith, A.D. (1996) Culture, Community and Territory: The Politics of Ethnicity and Nationalism. *Ethnicity and International Relations*, 72 (3) July, Blackwell Publishing on behalf of the Royal Institute of International Affairs, pp. 445-458.

[41] McHoul, A., Grace, W. (1995) *A Foucault primer: discourse, power and the subject*. Routledge, pp.73.

these bring into being inspiration for the actions, for the solutions of contemporary problems.

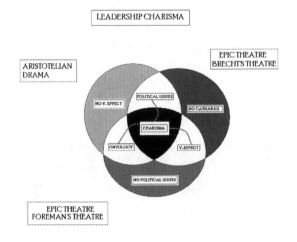

Image 1: Leadership Charisma

4. The Pragmatic Approach to the New Theory of Charismatic Leadership

4.1 Theatre and Politics and the process drama

When we talk about drama, we are trying to imagine ourselves in differing roles and situations; we are operating in a mode of 'as if'. Moreover, we are transforming our creative imagination into acts. The difference between real life and life as a drama is the mental process of being 'as if'. In addition, during the drama process we must acknowledge the fact of the actual world –as well as the fictional one which via our future actions may become reality.

> 'Drama is Being 'as if'. It is a total process, internal and external, that occurs when we transform our creative imagination into acts, (. . .) but life and drama are so alike that contemporary scholars can talk of the drama of life, or life as drama.'[42]

Are there differences between theatrical drama creation and political creation? Are we able to compare the drama created via the actor on a political stage—leader and the audience, with the theatrical arena? Drama is a process of creation; it is comparing the actual and fictional. It is the way how we think about new possibilities.[43] The

---

[42] Courtney, R. (1990) *Drama and Intelligence: A Cognitive Theory.* Montreal, McGill-Queen's University Press, pp.10.

[43] Ibid., pp.24.

world of drama and world of politics—is the world of 'as if'. Politics involves, as Harold Lasswell noticed, 'Who gets what, when and how'.[44] This little 'how'—is all about politicians, leaders who make people want to feel or be different from their everyday selves, who encourage them to believe in transformation: 'That's why I'm in this race. Not just to hold an office, but to gather with you to transform a nation.'[45]

My aim is to analyze Barack Obama's performance and speeches as an exceptional well developed drama process, a collaborative group power relation and movement which was created by Obama during the United States Presidential Election. Obama, the man who made history by becoming the first African-American President of the United States, by the drama process, creates an energizing movement which brought into being a fictional world of metaphors and signs based on the idea of American dream giving the meaning to himself—as first African-American who managed to fulfill the American dream and disprove the claim that the United States is a racist nation. Significantly, we need to notice the act of creation which took place between Obama and the other participants of the political drama during the last presidential run in United States. Hence meanings created between Obama and the participants of the drama could not be established in advance.

> 'The election of Mr. Obama amounted to a national catharsis—a repudiation of a historically unpopular Republican president and his economic and foreign policies, and an embrace of Mr. Obama's call for a change in the direction and the tone of the country. But it was just

---

[44]   Staudt, A., Weaver, W.G. (1997) *Political science & feminisms*. New York: Twayne Publishers, pp.135.

[45]   Obama, B., *Our Past, Future & Vision for America*, February 10, 2007, Obama Presidential Announcement Springfield, Illinois. [Internet] Available from; <http://obamaspeeches.com/>, [Accessed 29 August 2009].

as much a strikingly symbolic moment in the evolution of
the nation's fraught racial history '[46]

In addition to that quoted, it is crucial for the reasoning in this
study to define the meaning of the word 'drama', which evolved to
the Western culture, from the Ancient Greek, and rooted deeply in
the Greek verb *dran,* which means 'to do'.[47] Hence, as detailed by
Aristotle's *Poetics,* life consists of action, and its end is a mode of
action'.[48] Furthermore, Aristotle's concept of drama, declares that
the participants of the tragedy as a performance experience catharsis,
a certain state of being pleased or gratified by a moral or spiritual
cleansing. As noted by Kenneth Burke, these actions which lead to
the effect as catharsis are the same in a classic drama as well as in 'the
cheapest contemporary melodrama'.[49] Thus, are we able to site this
in the political, contemporary Obama's performances? This follows
the statements of Jacques Derrida and his claims that social actions
as well as dramatic actions never follow accepted practices. Moreover,
their existence strongly depends on two kinds of action, the first
being based on traditional practices and the second on a participant's
creativity.[50] Consequently, there is a possibility of connection
between the performances which are created on the theatrical
stage (understood as a scene, an area in which people are brought
together)[51] with the delivered in the political arena.

---

[46] Nagourney, A., Obama Elected President as Racial Barrier Falls,
November 4, 2008, *The New York Post* [Internet] Available from:
<http://www.nytimes.com/2008/11/05/us/politics/05elect.html>,
[Accessed 29 August 2009].

[47] McDonald, M., Walton, J.M. (2007) *The Cambridge companion to
Greek and Roman theatre.* Cambridge University Press, pp. 36.

[48] Aristotle, (2004) *Poetics.*Kessinger Publishing Co, pp.7.

[49] Burke, K. (1925) *Psychology and form.* The Dial.

[50] Rosenau, P.M. (1992) *Post-modernism and the Social Sciences.* Princeton:
Princeton UP.

[51] Elam, K. (1980) *The semiotics of theatre and drama.* Methuen
Publishing Ltd, pp.64.

4.2 Theatre and Politics and the Idea of Performance

Performance is the process of living, a process of assimilation. Moreover, it is the process of co-relations and the creation of the relationship with others. The theatrical performance along with the political, shares one aim—the creation of two worlds, a personal as well as the social. Thus, the process of performance depends on initiating an action which will lead the actor on the political stage, the leader on the theatrical one, or simply us, as human beings on the stage of life, from self presenting to the presentation of self in role.[52] Hence, Obama who presented himself as a senator from Illinois during the last Presidential Election in the United States moved himself into the role of an 'All American Hero', the first African-American who won the presidential elections and who has become the 'life sign' associated with the idea of the American Dream. Moreover, the new form, or costume created by the Obama image fulfilled the idea of the American Dream and gave the substance to his own words that 'America is a place where anything is possible'.[53]

In addition, the performer Obama had to raise crucial, ontological questions, which were closely related to the idea of 'being', especially the American nation being. His performance initiated the process of arousing certain emotions and feelings in the American Nation. Those emotions were closely attached to their knowledge and belief of what had been stated. Answering the questions 'who am I?' as an American individual, 'how can I change the vision of the United States?', and 'Am I able to change it?' This crucial in the process of the American Nation's electoral run participation.

---

[52] Goffman, E. (1959) *The presentation of self in everyday life,* Volume 174 of Doubleday anchor books Anchor books, Issue 2 of University of Edinburgh. Social Services Research Centre. Monograph. Doubleday.

[53] Ibid., (Obama, B., Acceptance speech)

'My father was a foreign student, born and raised in a small village in Kenya. He grew up herding goats, went to school in a tin-roof shack. His father, my grandfather, was a cook, a domestic servant.

But my grandfather had larger dreams for his son. Through hard work and perseverance my father got a scholarship to study in a magical place: America, which stood as a beacon of freedom and opportunity to so many who had come before. While studying here, my father met my mother. (. . .) My parents shared not only an improbable love; they shared an abiding faith in the possibilities of this nation. They would give me an African name, Barack, or 'blessed,' believing that in a tolerant America your name is no barrier to success. '[54]

Furthermore, the theatrical as well as the political performance is a process of making the impossible—possible, by trying out the 'not-really-real': the idea of the American Dream is there for what we need to consider as both an actual and a real. Hence, evolves the process of making somebody believe in an uncertain or provisionally grounded based hypothesis. In this same manner, Obama's political drama occurred, possessing the same, or almost the same, characteristics as the theatrical drama. Taking into consideration the political, created by the America's new president drama, we do not have sufficient power or resources to accomplish the explanation of the American Dream idea or 'we can do this' as a reality and a rational which occurs in the physical world. Nevertheless, Obama's dramatic performance managed to transform the American nation, and that transformation became an authentic, real fact, (yet based on unrealistic concepts). Obama's performance changed the American

---

[54]   Obama, B., *California Democratic National Convention Speech*, July 27, 2004. [Internet] Available from: <http://www.barackobama. com/2004/07/27/keynote_address_at_the_2004_de_1.php>, [Accessed 29 August 2009].

nation's attitudes in the real, actual world. 'President Obama spurred a dramatic change in the way whites think about African-Americans before he had even set foot in the Oval Office; (. . .). They call it the Obama Effect. '[55]

The created effect as charisma appears during the process of Obama's dramatic performance when the American electorate experiences his performance much as they do events in their own life. When Obama and the American Nation believe in the dramatic action (and, paradoxically, they do realise that it is merely fiction), they without conscious control, compare it with their life experience.

In addition, we may also comment on those who did not take an active part in Obama's performance. By distancing themselves from the American electoral run they were able to recognise a difference between Obama and the character in which he inhabited, between actual and fictional, and take note of their experience. In theatrical performance, especially in the epic theatre, the process of alienation is called—'the alienation effect'. The alienation effect is giving those who participate, and even if distancing themselves from the event, a deep meaning, leading to the accumulation of knowledge, hope and belief, that they 'we can do this', what ever the words 'can do this' means. What is worth acknowledging is the simple fact that the charisma in Obama's leadership depends on each individual participant of the drama process and his/her personal imagination of the 'we can do this' idea. 'That is the true genius of America, a faith in the simple dreams of its people, the insistence on small miracles.'[56]

---

[55] The Obama effect: Researchers cite President's role in reducing racism. Thursday, February 12, 2009—11:38, *Psychology & Sociology*. [Internet] Available from: <http://esciencenews.com/articles/2009/02/12/the. obama.effect.researchers.cite.presidents.role.reducing.racism>, [Accessed 29 August 2009].

[56] Ibid., (Obama, B., *Acceptance Speech*)

Obama's performance brought into being two different kinds of effect: 'transformation' and 'how to be'. Barack Obama as a future leader acts to change, or transform the American nation; this is a 'knowing how to do'.

> 'When I am president, I will sign a universal health care law by the end of my first term. My plan will cover the uninsured by letting people buy into the same kind of health care plan that members of Congress give themselves. (. . .)We can do this.'[57]

The initial effect of dramatic performance known as a transformation is changing the American nation's 'knowing'. The process of 'negotiation' and 'persuasion' appears. Obama's followers come to believe, not only that Barack Obama will be the true elected president in terms of created reforms and their effectiveness, but by adding 'we can do this', the American Nation comes to believe that there is a real and actual possibility of change. This kind of 'believing' is equivalent in connotation with 'knowing'. Gradually, the stage of drama called charisma appears—not only the leader's words sound possible but actually the believe 'we can do this'. The process of waking up the imagination of individuals comes into existence. There is now necessity to explain how Obama is planning to put through the steps of a prescribed legislative procedure, on account of the fact that each of Obama's drama participants heard the 'we can do this' quotation which could act as a catalyst or determine the form that a positive emotional reaction takes place.

> 'We should briefly note that emotions tend, under certain conditions, to block or encourage specific elements of the dramatic model. The player who says, "I can't do that" when engaged in a specific dramatic task is usually reacting to some deep-seated fear. '[58]

---

[57] Ibid., (Obama, B. *Turn the page speech*)
[58] Ibid., pp.53.

We may assume that the opposite statement, to 'we can do this' ('we can't do this' quoted above) avoids the effect of memorising and reacting to some traumatic past experience. Moreover, we may assume that the opposite statement, to 'we can do this' avoids the effect of memorising and reacting to some traumatic past experience. Creating the spirit that improved the American Nation's ability to face the fear of deeply rooted critical experiences.

4.3 A New Explanation of the External World

'When I am president, I will sign a universal health care law by the end of my first term. My plan will cover the uninsured by letting people buy into the same kind of health care plan that members of Congress give themselves. It will bring down costs by investing in information technology, and preventative care, and by stopping the drug companies from price-gouging when patients need their medicine.'[59]

To make the process of the American nation's transformation accessible, the political Obama's dramatic performance needs to provide the people with an explanation of the external world. The new explanation is a fictional one—in the distant future it may become a reality. Essentially the issue, as to how their leader is going to bring about or perform those changes and reforms is left to the American Nation's imagination. Ironically, with Obama's creation the American Nation is able to move along its knowledge. Following Benedetto Croce, there are two kinds of knowledge, intuitive knowledge and the logical one. The first is acquired through the process of imagination, which leads to the production of images and the second is that obtained through the intellect, which serves as a route to the creation of concepts. The battle between Barack Obama and Hillary Clinton had been a 'fight' which woke up those two

---

[59]   Ibid., (Obama, B. *Turn the page speech*)

kinds of imagination which in Obama's case led to the production of images, contrary to Clinton's which served as a route for concepts. Furthermore, the American Nation as a player, or participant in the political drama, and the leader, Barack Obama, will consider the fiction as an alternative to the real world. In each of these Obama's actions, the American Nation via its imagination and future actions may give the reality to it. They are giving that statement 'we can do this', a meaning which has been perceived by them before. Furthermore, Immanuel Kant argues that imagination is crucial for putting together into order and structures one's phenomena of past experiences into the process of perceiving.[60] In the political drama, the act of exchanging takes places in a leader's—Obama's imagination, as well as the American Nation's imagination. Moreover, the process of Obama's performance brought into existence the ways in which both sides perceive the ontological essence of existence. The performance of the leader, (Obama) in a political drama, moves the American Nation not so much by abolishing the idea of the actual, real world but by dulling their awareness of the idea of a new, imagined world. 'We can do this (. . .) And it reminds us of a simple truth (. . .) a truth you carry by being here today—that in the face of impossible odds, people who love their country can change it. '[61] The Obama performance works only when the new, fictional world is considered by the Americans seriously and imagined as a real, possible world. In addition, this possible world can offer a reason for the active participation.

4.4 Contract of Trust

Obama as a leader and his followers, both drama players need to have confidence in the truth, worth, and reliability of each other. In dramatic actions it is a so called 'fiduciary contract'. Barack Obama

---

[60] Furlong, E.J. (2004) *Imagination.* Volume 7 of Muirhead library of philosophy. Routledge, pp.117.

[61] Ibid., (Obama, B. *Turn the page speech*)

and the American Nation without doubts or reservation make a mutually satisfactory agreement. 'The fiduciary contract is the operational foundation for all those actions inherently dramatic in nature: storytelling, debate, dialogue, negotiation, and the like.'[62]

The agreement of trust, or the fiduciary contract begins when a leading figure of the political drama—here Obama and the American Nation entrust themselves to two positions: 'the vaunt' and 'the proposition'. The vaunt, was Obama's Presidential Announcement which introduced his candidacy for President, and the proposition, the plan suggested for Acceptance, both begin Obama's political drama.

> 'Let me begin by saying thanks to all you who've traveled, from far and wide, to brave the cold today. We all made this journey for a reason. It's humbling, but in my heart I know you didn't come here just for me, you came here because you believe in what this country can be. '[63]

When Obama initiated the vaunt, and the American Nation, responded the dramatic context was established. Obama's initial proposition suggests that he possesses knowledge, understanding, or certain information. 'I recognize there is a certain presumptuousness—a certain audacity—to this announcement. I know I haven't spent a lot of time learning the ways of Washington. But I've been there long enough to know that the ways of Washington must change.'[64] Moreover, it began the dramatic action. He as candidate for the American Presidency formally requested the American Nation to react positively or favourably—an intention to, or having the power to, induce an action or a belief statement to which both players (Obama and the American Nation) could

---

[62] Ibid., pp.32.

[63] Ibid., (Obama, B. *Our Past, Future & Vision for America*)

[64] Ibid., (Obama, B. *Our Past, Future & Vision for America*)

addressed themselves; only after the announcement, did the dramatic meaning move to a deeper level.

The most important skills or mechanisms for the evolution of co-operation between the leader as Obama and his followers (the American Nation) are: desiring (wanting) and negotiation. Obama in the role of candidate for the American Presidency had to express or state indirectly some provocations, so called 'temptations' as well as cause to believe, or convince, the other players of the political drama, to move the action forward on its own terms. But also what is very important is the satisfaction sufficient to meet a demand or requirement to the American Nation.

Obama's acts are socially significant, and thereby they construct social reality.

In politics, especially in political drama, believing in a new, created fictional world, which can become actual in the future, depends on the social rather than logical and rational mood of the Obama's speeches and performance. This expresses an intention to influence other participants' behaviour.

> 'Perhaps a new spirit is rising among us. If it is, let us trace its movements and pray that our own inner being may be sensitive to its guidance, for we are deeply in need of a new way beyond the darkness that seems to close around us.'[65]

> 'We must find a way to come together in this country—to realize that the responsibility we have to one another as Americans is greater than the pursuit of any ideological

---

[65] King, M.L. Speech, Riverside Church, April 4, 1967.[Internet] Available from: <http://letterfromhere.blogspot.com/2009/01/perhaps-new-spirit-is-rising-among-us.html>, [Accessed 29 August 2009].

agenda or corporate bottom line. Democrats of California,
it's time to turn the page.'[66]

Moreover, the fictional but significant world can change what the American nation perceives, knows, and believes and this leads to the process of transformation. The difference between the actual America and the fictional one lies in its attitude to actuality. The new Obama's fictional world carries a historical and cultural context. Hence, the American Nation did not think deeply about Obama's performance. By watching, and being the witness only, they were taking active part in this drama. We need to address this question, 'If we ever inhabit the fictional?'. Coleridge argues 'that the reader should willingly suspend disbelief in order to release any sense of incredulity and let the imagination, 'this shadow, run free (. . .) in the story and thus fully absorb the narrative and character in a given poem or play'.[67] Conversely, the American Nation may consider the new created fictional world as true and something that is possible in reality.

4.5 The Speeches of Barack Obama

"Politics is a fascinating game"[68] (H. Truman)—a game which needs players. To be able to understand dramatic fiction in political drama created between Obama and his followers we need to approach the Obama's speeches in this same way that is how we analyse a theatrical drama or a piece of poetry. We have to remember about the meanings which a leader and his followers, or participants, of dramatic relationship share. Moreover, we have to remember about the possible meaning which can be created between them. To make

---

[66] Ibid., (Obama, B. *Turn the page speech*)

[67] Ferri, A.J. (2007) *Willing suspension of disbelief: poetic faith in film.* Lexington Books, pp.103.

[68] Truman.H.S., Hillman W., Mr. President: The First Publication from the Personal Diaries, Private Letters, Papers and Revealing Interviews of Harry S. Truman, pp.198.

people understand his new message, he had to transform his speeches into a pattern the American Nation recognised from its past. Thus the recipients are able to imagine, this as personal experience which derives from acquiring and remembering sensual impressions, as memories. And as Wildon Carr argues which are brought together again more or less fantastically.[69] Elements of the fiction are the substance of imagination. For this reason it is essential for this paper to acknowledge the fact and meaning of the American Dream and the 'we can do this' statement, which for the American Nation, by recalling the positive memories from its past, have such significant meaning.

4.6 The American Dream and Dr. Martin Luther King

'I say to you today, my friends, that in spite of the difficulties and frustrations of the moment, I still have a dream. It is a dream deeply rooted in the American dream.

I have a dream that one day this nation will rise up and live out the true meaning of its creed: 'We hold these truths to be self-evident: that all men are created equal.'(. . .)

I have a dream that my four children will one day live in a nation where they will not be judged by the colour of their skin but by the content of their character.

I have a dream today.' (Dr Martin Luther King)[70]

---

[69] Fawcett, E.D. (1939) *Oberland dialogues*. Macmillan and Co., Limited, pp.43.

[70] King, M.L, I have a dream speech, August 28, 1963, Washington. [Internet] Available from: <http://www.mlkonline.net/dream.html>, [Accessed 29 August 2009].

In the American tradition the American Dream is a promise of success, fame and wealth for those who work hard. Moreover, it is a promise of a better, happier, richer and equal life. Also, in the twenty first century, this idea remains a major element of the American Nation identity. Many nations identify themselves with a language, blood, or shared history. The American Nation was crucially a 'creation of the collective imagination'[71].

'Twenty-five years ago Martin Luther King had a dream of an America where men and women would be judged not on the color of their skin but on the content of their character," Mr. Rudd said. "Today what America has done is turn that dream into a reality.'[72]

4.7 Barack Obama's Story

'His story is the American story—values from the heartland, a middle-class upbringing in a strong family, hard work and education as the means of getting ahead, and the conviction that a life so blessed should be lived in service to others.'[73]

Barack Obama, the 44th President of the United States, was elected on November 4, 2008, and sworn in on January 20, 2009. As previously stated his, life story fulfilled the idea of the American Dream. To disseminate the Barack Obama meteoric rise:

---

[71] Ibid., pp.6.

[72] Malkin, B., Barack Obama has made Martin Luther King's dream a reality, Telegraph. 11:14AM GMT 05 Nov 2008. [Internet] Available from: <http://www.telegraph.co.uk/news/worldnews/>, [Accessed 29 August 2009].

[73] The White House. [Internet] Available from: <http://www.whitehouse.gov/administration/President_Obama/>, [Accessed 29 August 2009].

Barack Obama, African-American, born in Hawaii in August 4, 1961, was brought up, in a middle class family, by his grandparents. After his hard work through school and further education, he managed to move to Chicago. There he worked with several churches, helping their communities. After a while, attended law school, where he became the first African-American President of the Harvard Law Review. Upon graduation, Barack Obama lectured law at the University of Chicago, and from 1997 to 2004 served three terms in the Illinois Senate.

> "Barack Obama is on the verge of making the American dream a reality"[74]

In February 2007, he began his run for the Presidency and in the 2008 Democratic Presidential Primaries won his party nomination against Hillary Rodham Clinton. He defeated John McCain (Republican) and on January 20, 2009 was inaugurated as the first African-American President of the United States.[75]

'The dream of Martin Luther King Jr. has become a reality in the life of Barack Obama'[76]

In addition, we need to acknowledge a crucial aspect of the Obama's performance. He used his past—a past in which he could utilise elements of the 'educational drama', or so called 'creative drama': 'An improvisational, non-exhibitional, process-centered form of drama in which participants are guided by a leader to imagine, enact and

---

[74] Miller, S., *US elections 2008: Why Barack Obama epitomizes the American dream.* Helium. [Internet] Available from: <http://www.helium.com/items/1215419-us-elections-2008-why-barack-obama-epitomizes-the-american-dream>, [Accessed 29 August 2009].

[75] Ibid.,

[76] Ibid.,

reflect upon human experiences'.[77] Creative drama is 'anything which involves persons in active role-taking situations in which attitudes, not characters, are the chief concerns'.[78] The holistic performance, created by Obama and the American Nation, was an improvisation based on Obama's story, the story of his life and encompassing the American Nation story—the American Dream ('an idea that shaped a nation')[79]. That was a baseline for action, reflection and the imagination, of both sides (Obama and the American Nation), to succesfully create the drama as the visionary charismatic leadership process.

In this kind of drama the leader is not the source of answers. Obama did not command the American Nation as to what it should do. The American Nation is encuraged to find their own voice, immerse themselves in roles and create their own meaning.[80] The American Nation was, and still is, responsible for their 'here and now' as well as their future choices, actions, and automatically their own life. What connects the presidential campaign in the United States with the creative/educational drama is the complete improvisation from its participants. The American Nation was not supplied with any kind of script, which showed them directions, or how to act or behave.

---

[77] Wagner, B.J. (1999) *Building moral communities through educational drama*. Greenwood Publishing Group, pp.3.

[78] Heathcote, D. (1977). Drama as challenge. In J. Hodgson (Ed.). *The uses of drama: Acting as a social and educational force*. London: Eyre Methuen, pp.43.

[79] Cullen, J. (2004) The American dream: a short history of an idea that shaped a nation. Oxford University Press.

[80] Brennan, R. (2008) *Educational drama: A tool for promoting marketing learning?*
Middlesex University, and Glenn Pearce, University of Western Sydney. [Internet] Available from: <http://www-new1.heacademy.ac.uk/assets/bmaf/documents/publications/IJME/accepted_for_publication/IJME237.pdf>, [Accessed 29 August 2009].

The essential part of the creative or educational drama is the participants' (the American Nation and Obama) creation, where there are playing themselves in a dramatic setting (time, place, and circumstance in which narrative drama [where the focus is on the story] takes place)[81]. In addition, the action has its beginning and its focus on the story. The tutor, or the conductor of the drama, or the leader in politics, is responsible for the creation of the story. Obama was the one who arranged and performed events which gave the pretext for the American Nation drama—the Presidential run in the United States. It is essential to present the Obama's life story in his own words.

> 'I live in Chicago now, but I am not a native of that great city. I moved there when I was just a year out of college, and a group of churches offered me a job as a community organizer so I could help rebuild neighborhoods that had been devastated by the closing of steel plants.
>
> The salary was $12,000 a year plus enough money to buy an old, beat-up car, and so I took the job and drove out to Chicago, where I didn't know a soul. And during the time I was there, we worked to set up job training programs for the unemployed and after school programs for kids.
>
> And it was the best education I ever had, because I learned in those neighborhoods that when ordinary people come together, they can achieve extraordinary things.
>
> After three years, I went back to law school. I left there with a degree and a lifetime of debt, but I turned down the corporate job offers so I could come back to Chicago and organize a voter registration drive. I also started a civil rights practice, and began to teach constitutional law.

---

[81] Stauffer, R.M. (1927) *The progress of drama, through the centuries.* Macmillan.

And after a few years, people started coming up to me and telling me I should run for state Senate. So I did what every man does when he's faced with a big decision—I prayed, and I asked my wife. And after consulting those two higher powers, I decided to get in the race.

And everywhere I'd go, I'd get two questions. First, they'd ask, "Where'd you get that funny name, Barack Obama?" Because people just couldn't pronounce it. They'd call me "Alabama," or they'd call me "Yo Mama." And I'd tell them that my father was from Kenya, and that's where I got my name. And my mother was from Kansas, and that's where I got my accent from.

And the second thing people would ask me was, "You seem like a nice young man. You've done all this great work. You've been a community organizer, and you teach law school, you're a civil rights attorney, you're a family man—why would you wanna go into something dirty and nasty like politics?"

And I understand the question, and the cynicism. We all understand it.

We understand it because we get the sense today that politics has become a business and not a mission. In the last several years, we have seen Washington become a place where keeping score of who's up and who's down is more important than who's working on behalf of the American people.'[82]

4.8 Storytelling

Taking into consideration Barack Obama's performance and his drama, we need to notice how effective a storyteller he is. Continually following his speeches, the American Nation came face to face with

---

[82]   Ibid., (Obama, B. *Turn the page speech*)

two ways of perceiving the reality—as from the old belief position and the new one. The old belief:

> 'And the second thing people would ask me was, "You seem like a nice young man. You've done all this great work. You've been a community organizer, and you teach law school, you're a civil rights attorney, you're a family man—why would you wanna go into something dirty and nasty like politics?'[83]

and the new perspective:

> 'And so the American people are hungry for a different kind of politics—the kind of politics based on the ideals this country was founded upon. The idea that we are all connected as one people. That we all have a stake in one another.'[84]

The time yet to come will establish the certainty or validity of first or second perspective. 'It was Bush's mess. Now it's becoming Obama's mess to average voters.'[85] But, even as the above example point out that the American nation came back to its former state, the actual participation of taking part in Obama's performance and accumulated knowledge, would have transform the nation. The ontological ability of the Obama's performance acts so effectively via pointing the way 'how to be', by which the American Nation may grasp the nature of being. Furthermore, there is a need to understand one crucial aspect of drama; the aim of Obama's performance was to change the way 'how', not 'what' the American Nation believe, expect or

---

[83] Ibid., (Obama, B. *Turn the page speech*)

[84] Ibid., (Obama, B. *Turn the page speech*)

[85] Tomsky, M. Obama administration. Michael Tomasky's blog, Thursday 13 August 2009. [Internet] Available from: <http://www.guardian.co.uk/commentisfree/michaeltomasky+world/obama-administration>, [Accessed 29 August 2009].

reflect. Thus, a result or effect of the Obama's performance, is not only the change in his followers' attitudes to this particular first African-American taking part in the presidential election, but the change in all forms of stereotypical thinking. 'More significantly, the election's outcome has disproved the claim that the United States is a racist nation, and that irrational racial animosities trump all other issues.'[86] 'Barack Hussein Obama was elected the 44th president of the United States on Tuesday, sweeping away the last racial barrier in American politics with ease as the country chose him as its first black chief executive.'[87] 'The election (and now the inauguration) of Barack Obama has inspired a widespread sense of awe at the scope and scale of change in race relations in America—and more than a hint of self-congratulation.'[88]

4.9 Barack Obama's Drama and the Metaphor

The American Dream has metaphorical connotations and takes its place in the Barack Obama's performance to dramatise the meaning of America. We may consider the 'Dream' as the extension of America. It is a mask or a costume or a thin veneer in a land which is able to keep alive this fiction. Make the dream real and actual, is what Obama awakens with his performance.

---

[86]   The election of Barack Obama, 5 November 2008. World Socialist Website. [Internet] Available from: <http://www.wsws.org/articles/2008/nov2008/pers-n05.shtml>, [Accessed 29 August 2009].

[87]   Nagourney, A. (2008) Obama Elected President as Racial Barrier Falls, November 4, *The New York Post.*[Internet] Available from: <http://www.nytimes.com/2008/11/05/us/politics/05elect.html>, [Accessed 29 August 2009].

[88]   Pascoe, P., *The Election of Barack Obama and the Politics of Interracial and Same-Sex Marriage.* Beekman Professor of Pacific and Northwest History and Professor of Ethnic Studies, University of Oregon) [Internet] Available from: <http://hnn.us/articles/60057.html>, [Accessed 29 August 2009].

'If there is anyone out there who still doubts that America is a place where all things are possible; who still wonders if the dream of our founders is alive in our time; who still questions the power of our democracy, tonight is your answer.'[89]

The metaphorical context of the drama brought a deeper level to the dramatic relation between Obama and the rest of the participants. The rationality—in other words, the personal, realistic actual meaning of the essence which stands by the world—dream (better healthcare system, better educational system, the end of war in Iraq) is always very individual and based on a fictional, but which via future actions may become actual and real. Dramatic metaphors in Obama's speeches and performances lead to a dramatic progress, where is a place for reasoning more than in a one-to-one relationship. There is a place for each individual of the American Nation to give their personal and rational meaning to the idea of the American Dream. This kind of intellectual reasoning, which derives from the metaphors, that appears in Obama's speeches and actions, become a psychological, or symbolic configuration or pattern of elements so unified as a whole that its properties cannot be derived from a simple summation of its parts and give the holistic picture of the process as charismatic political drama.

'I have a dream today. (. . .) I still have a dream. It is a dream deeply rooted in the American dream. I have a dream that one day this nation will rise up and live out the true meaning of its creed: "We hold these truths to be self-evident: that all men are created equal'.[90]

---

[89] Ibid., (Obama, B. *Election Night Victory Speech*)

[90] King, M.L. I have a dream speech. August 28, 1963, from the steps of the Lincoln Memorial. [Internet] Available from: <http://www.presentationhelper.co.uk/martin_luther_king_speech.htm>, [Accessed 29 August 2009].

5. How Does the Aristotelian and Educational Drama Manifest Itself in the Barack Obama's Charismatic Leadership? Conclusion.

Where does Barack Obama create the difference between the theatrical drama and the political drama? Can it be called a charismatic one? Essentially, the specific point or element that distinguishes one drama from the other is the relation of the one who delivers—Obama—and the receiver—the American Nation. We may observe, that both dramas are closely related by their unique participants' relation—which is so intense, indeed, in terms of theatrical drama each of them attempts to identify with the other and see things from that person's perspective: fit into the actors' or performers' shoes. The way in which the performer or the actor in a theatre manifests their interpretation of the role, or so called part of the play, and expresses it during the drama process is essentially closely related to others visions or expectations (director, leader). Furthermore, the performer needs to operate in a certain frame that constricts their ability to improvise. Significantly, for the theatrical drama is the identification and empathy of the players (the deliverer as well as the receiver), which observe carefully or critically each other trying to see from the others perspective. Therefore, dramatic action as mentioned above relies on mutuality, trust, and the fiduciary contract. The element that differentiates ordinary drama from the charismatic one is the interpretation of the meaning, which is shared in the charismatic process participations. The creator of charismatic leadership needs to be able to operate on different levels of created fiction. Everything depends on the leader's interpretation and his/her ability to support their acts with statements that need to have a factual, positive and real connotation with the other participants' imagination. This is brought into being by recalling the past meaningful and significant experiences. In this sense we may follow that Derrida's deconstruction is simply what the charismatic drama in terms of Obama's performance allows for the creation of meaning. That is what the participants (the American Nation) will 'fill in'. The authentic meaning of Obama's speech lies in the wide difference in ideas, which are created by the players\participants' imagination, here via Obama's speech interpretation and performance. The essence created between the players (the leader and the participants of the charismatic drama) is the creation of new ideas and future possibilities. Dramatisation in the process of charismatic leadership creation may be a major tool for instilling the values of co-operation between the nation as only supported by the leader's plans that are perceived as realistic. Furthermore, we must take into consideration the aims of the participants of the political drama when discussing charisma. These are mostly individual. The issue of the country, as history shows in most of the cases is less important than the private one. 'I'm in. And I'm in to win.'[91]—as sited by Hillary Clinton so essentially. We are hoping that there are leaders who meant when they said; 'That's why I'm in this race. Not just to hold an office, but to gather with you to transform a nation.'[92] In addition, as well as the leader's aims, there are also the private aims of the other co-players, which, as Obama's charismatic leadership shows, leads to the fact of suspended belief in the whole process perceived as charisma, and this disbelief may create the effect of confusion and misunderstanding from the leader's as well as the participants' point of view. Obama, as history shows, was not able to fulfil the dreams of each of the participants of the whole process as charisma. We need to address

---

[91] Clinton, H.R., Announcement to Run for U.S. President, Jan. 20, 2007. [Internet] Available from: <http://www.msnbc.msn.com/id/16720167/>, [Accessed 29 August 2009].

[92] Ibid., (Obama, B. *Our Past, Future & Vision for America*)

the question—'Is the leader ever able to fulfil the dreams of the each individual from the nation?' The answer to that question is—'No, the leader is not able to fulfil the dreams of the whole nation—as long as the aims of the leader differ from those who receive them.

In summary, drama is a total process of transformation. Moreover, it is the process of searching for and finding the answers to the questions—'Who am I?' Taking into consideration the Obama performance, we may notice that his drama differs somehow from the Aristotelian one. Hence, Aristotelian drama leads the participants to 'step into the actor's (in a theatre) or leader's (in politics) shoes'. Furthermore, we are trying to understand the leader's behaviour and if we do agree with his/her idea of the future possible world, the effect of following his/her leadership appears. However, in the drama as the charismatic leadership, the process of adhering with the leader's concepts and ideas becomes hindered, by the so called alienation effect, which links the drama as charisma to the epic theatre, and which so essentially expressed by Obama's own words; 'But this campaign that we're running has to be about your hopes, and your dreams, and what you will do.'

6. The Pragmatic Approach to the Charismatic Leadership Epic Theatre Approach

'My plays have to be properly performed if they are to be effective, so that for the sake of (oh! dear me) a non-Aristotelian dramaturgy I had to outline (calamity!) an epic theatre. (B. Brecht)'[93]

Let us closer examine, the connection between the drama and the epic theatre mechanism, which in addition to the dramatic, brought in the assumptions of this paper the effect of Barack Obama's charismatic leadership. As highlighted before, the main mechanism, which links Obama's dramatic performance, to the epic theatre was the alienation effect. Its creator Bertolt Brecht explored the idea of the alienation effect.[94] Moreover, Brecht's idea was to fulfil the idea of drama with real plays. This takes into consideration the political and social issues.

In contrary, the dramatic part of his speeches are responsible for rousing up the participants' imagination and leading them into the fictional world, the so called 'as if (. . .) '; the alienation effect is responsible for setting aside any kind of illusion. Obama during his performances, as an 'actor' on a political stage, who created his image as an American hero, the first future African-American President, made it obvious that he is the one whom 'everyone is looking at and listening to'. Hence, the mechanisms of epic theatre was working

---

[93]   Mumford, M. (2009) *Bertolt Brecht.*Taylor & Francis.
[94]   Ibid., pp.65.

against the notion of the so called 'forth wall', which in a fictional way exist between the audience and the performer.[95] Moreover, the erection of this kind of fictional wall does not allowed the actor to behave in a way as if he is a character and as if the audience is not present.[96] Even so, it does not mean that their intellectually, imaginative experience is brought together or closer to each other. On the contrary Brecht wanted to 'disrupt' his audience mentally and wake up their opinions about the participated performance. Thus, his aim was to avoid "catharsis"[97] within the audience, where else Aristotelian drama leads to it. We may assume, that if the process of bringing up those opposite techniques will lead the performance, being constructed in this way, to the emotional purification, as well as allowing the creation of independent, personal meaning by each of its participants. But how does this technique express itself in an Obama speech, in him and in performance, which he creates.

To pay attention to Obama and his own story. We do know that he is the first African-American who won the Presidential Election in the United States. His own life, his own personal story, and the history of America led him to victory. His presidential campaign image, the role in which he was performing, was his own life story, only put in the process of drama. Using his own 'skin' as a costume he managed to establish the baseline for his campaign's scenario. Accordingly, to the epic theatre, where the actor needs to keep a certain distance from the performed character, Obama in a natural way managed to keep that distance. He did not have to perform a character role—it was him. His life was the story of the dreams of those who voted for him. 'But

[95]   Rouse, J. (1984) Brecht and the Contradictory Actor, *Theatre Journal*, 36 (1) Mar., The Interpretive Actor, pp.25-42.

[96]   Gray, R.D. (1976) *Brecht the Dramatist*. New York: Cambridge University Press.

[97]   Kaufmann, H. (1973) *Social psychology: the study of human interaction*. Holt, Rinehart and Winston, pp.378.

my grandfather had larger dreams for his son'[98]—by saying this, in a natural way 'I have a dream today'[99] started something in the memory and emotions of the American Nation. Only Obama, during the presidential run in the United States was able to express and perform those few words in the most natural and inartificial way. He was able to fulfil the Brechtian ideas not to go in deep into the character— in Obama's case, Martin Luther King.[100] By this reasoning, he has become the twenty first century image of the past prominent leader, in a natural way without imitating or assimilating with him. Obama was playing himself only in dramatic setting (in this case Presidential Election in the United States). Thus, we may assume that in the same way as in the epic theatre, Obama's performance or assimilation with this part of his life is contradictory the Stanislavsky concept of acting.[101] This depends on complete transformation into another type of person. 'Usually the actor does not succeed for long in really feeling like the other person' (Brecht)[102]. Hence, in the creative process of charismatic leadership, personality, and past experience is of the high importance.

6.1 Barack Obama's Speeches and Performance in the Light of the Alienation Effect.

In this section, Barack Obama's oratory and performance are going to be scrutinised systematically from the alienation effect perspective.

---

[98]   Ibid., (Obama, B., *California Democratic National Convention Speech*, July 27, 2004)

[99]   Ibid.,(King, M.L, *I Have a Dream Speech*)

[100]   Kirk, J.A. (2005) *Martin Luther King Jr.Profiles in power.* Pearson Education.

[101]   Whyman, R. (2008) *The Stanislavsky system of acting: legacy and influence in modern performance.* Cambridge University Press.

[102]   Brecht, B., Bentley, E. (1961) On Chinese Acting. *The Tulane Drama Review*, 6 (1) September, The MIT Press Stable, pp. 130-136. [Internet] Available from: <http://www.jstor.org/stable/1125011>, [Accessed 29 August 2009].

The alienation effect as explained in the first section of this paper (chapter 3.1 of this paper), as the 'instant of intrusion into the everyday. (. . .) It is what constantly demands to be explained and re-explained. '[103] We need to address the question, 'what in the actual political world reminds the estrangement which needs to be explored over and over again?' We may assume that any new way of performing or presenting political statements (healthcare, education) during any kind of campaign (presidential) need to be reinvestigated and expressed, by future, possible leaders in the mode of Obama— in the way to make the nation understand the 'old issues', from a different perspective. What is crucial, in terms of the epic theatre as well as the charismatic leadership, is the interpersonal nation's perspective not the leader's.

6.2 The Alienation Effect in Barack Obama's speeches and the Effect as Charismatic Visionary Leadership.

Following the notes, which Bertolt Brecht left us, to analyse or create this kind of alienation effect, reveals the deeper meaning of those so-called metaphorical sentences such as, 'It's time to turn the page', 'and the American Dream' or 'We can do this'. Asides such as:

> 'I come away with an unyielding belief that if we only had a government as responsible as all of you, as compassionate as the American people, that there is no obstacle that we can't overcome. There is no destiny that we cannot fulfil.'[104]

are 'empty' in any kind of substance or essence from the political, or economical point of view, but means everything for the American nation and their history, their past and present. The above sentences

---

[103]   Jameson, F. (2000) *Brecht and method*. Verso, pp.84.

[104]   Obama, B., Manassas, Prince William County, Virginia November 3, 2008, 10:30pm—Night Before the Election speech. [Internet] Available from: <http://obamaspeeches.com/>, [Accessed 29 August 2009].

from Obama's speeches, in the same way as metaphors brought, the alienation effect into existence.

Analysing Obama's oratory from the point of the Aristotelian drama, we may assume that those sentences or asides led to the process of 'waking up' the imagination of the American Nation. Moreover, analysing this same speech from the epic theatre point of view, these same statements followed by the further text of high political importance, (statements about medical care, war in Iraq, all economical issue so crucial in terms of future reforms and the United States well being), when merged together (as we may observe below) in Obama's speeches, the moment of performing them brings the alienation effect into existence.

> 'It's time to turn the page on health care—to bring together unions and businesses, Democrats and Republicans, and to let the insurance and drug companies know that while they get a seat at the table, they don't get to buy every chair. (. . .)

> 'It's time to turn the page on education—to move past the slow decay of indifference that says some schools can't be fixed and some kids just can't learn.'[105]

In addition, the power of alienation makes the participants perceive the well known 'old issues' in their personal and individual way. Hence, the leader, as Obama by using the technique of alienation was able to 'bring about some understanding of frequent and quite ordinary operations (. . .) by illuminating (them) in a special way.'[106] The word 'illuminating' is so crucial. Its justifies the simple fact, that during a political campaign there are no innovative ways of dealing with the old issues, there are only some new concepts which can help to' resell the old product'.

---

[105] Ibid., (Obama, B. *Turn the page speech*)
[106] Ibid., pp.84.

In summary,

> 'Hence, the celebrated Verfremdungseffekt [alienation effect] to prevent the audience from entering too deeply into the illusion of the drama. [. . .] Through such techniques, the audience was to be sufficiently

detached from the action to pronounce moral judgment upon it. '[107]

Conclusion:

a) The alienation effect was preventing the American Nation from totally embracing the fictional world created by Obama speeches, because of their hesitant interpretation of the real and the actual.

b) In contrary The America Nation was not forced to create its own moral judgment upon its past experiences linked to the past disappointing politics or leader's statements.

In epic theatre especially in Foreman's model[108] but unlikely in Brecht's Theatre which was interested in political or social concerns, Foreman adapted the alienation effect to perform the ontological issues.[109] Thus, to analyse the Obama performance, as charismatic leadership, we need to take into consideration one more element— the ontological ("to force people to another level of conscious" so that creative solutions are possible)[110] In addition to consider the American Nation forgetting the past negative political experiences:

---

[107] Cohn, R. (1982) *New American Dramatists: 1960-1080*. New York: The MacMillan Presss Ltd, pp.28-29.

[108] Roose-Evans, J. (1984) *Experimental theatre from Stanislavsky to Peter Brook*, Routledge.

[109] Ibid., p.59.

[110] Shank, T. (2002) *Beyond the boundaries: American alternative theatre*. University of Michigan Press, pp.161.

'And so the American people are hungry for a different kind of politics—the kind of politics based on the ideals this country was founded upon. The idea that we are all connected as one people. That we all have a stake in one another.'[111]

The visionary Obama statements about the process of reform (medical care, education) need to be linked to the very positive and metaphorical statements such as, 'It's time to turn the page'[112] which 'woke up' the American Nation imagination and this process led to new images and creation of political possibilities via the imagination of the American electorate.

In summary, we may be able to say that Obama's performance, based on the text of his speeches, brought into being the expression of the American nation's highest emotions—which we are able to compare to 'catharsis'[113]. However, the effect as catharsis is not equal to the one called charisma. Hence, the baseline for Obama's charismatic leadership was the essence of catharsis—an emotional purging. But of the higher importance is the bringing about of the illusion of how strong and innovative the Obama vision is. In addition, Obama was able to create a vision about how to perceive resolutions vital to the United States' economical, medical and educational crises. We are able to call his leadership a visionary one. Beyond what has been stated, the Obama's vision was the facto American nation's fictional and illusionary vision of the new, future and better world. I conclude, as stated at the beginning of this paper, that Obama's leadership is a 'visionary leadership where the vision is co-created by the participants with the leader as a conductor of this relationship.'[114]

---

[111] Ibid., (Obama, B., *California Democratic National Convention Speech*, July 27, 2004)

[112] Ibid., (Obama, B. *Turn the page speech*)

[113] Ibid., pp.251.

[114] Ibid., (2nd chapter of this paper)

Charismatic Leadership Components:

- Leader of the charismatic leadership/drama—deliverer

- Participant—receivers

- Alienation effect / Foucault's technology of individualisation

- Drama 'praxis' ('to do') and its ontological issues

- Political issues and concerns

7. Justification of Thesis

7.1 The Measure of Emotional Response (October 2008, AdSam Presidential Survey)[115]

> 'Voters' attitudes toward a politician are influenced by the kinds of emotions that are evoked repeatedly by his behaviour. This finding suggest that one source of the emotions identified as important determinants of attitudes and voting behaviour (Kinder & Abelson)'[116]

Emotional experience is the key part of the voters' experience. AdSam ascertained the dimensions, which give the precise measure of people's emotional response to a 'candidates position on the issues'[117], the so called 'Emotional Temperature'.[118] During the last Presidential Elections in the United States, AdSam measured how strongly voters felt about their candidates, and what level of emotional engagement they perceived towards them. Hillary Clinton, as the results shows, was not able to create an emotional connection with the voters (93-70 on the scale, where 173 is how emotionally positive voters say they would like to feel about a candidate). Furthermore, Obama produced as a result of his relationship with the voters the highest

---

[115] SenseUs Emotional Response Polling. [Internet] Available from: <http://senseus.net/file_download/27>, [Accessed 29 August 2009].

[116] Clark, E.M., Brock, T.C., Stewart, B.D. (1994) *Attention, attitude, and affect in response to advertising*. Lawrence Erlbaum Associates, pp.242.

[117] Ibid.,

[118] Ibid.,

emotional response (Democrats 120 and Independents 97) where else Clinton managed to generate—97 among Democrats and McCain 81– among Independents.

> 'Most polls measure only the participant's rationale responses, which only reveals half the story. Every human response is a combination of rational and emotional processing.'[119]

How do Voters Emotionally Connect with the Candidates' Positions on Key Issues? AdSam Emotional Temperature[120]

> '**ADSAM Emotional Temperature**—visually shows how the emotional strengths are ranked for different segments. A formula is added to the emotional strength to normalize the data and create an index that makes the different segments comparable. Rank orders are obtained by relating all scores to 100 as the average score.'

---

[119] Ibid., pp.3.
[120] Ibid., pp.3-13.

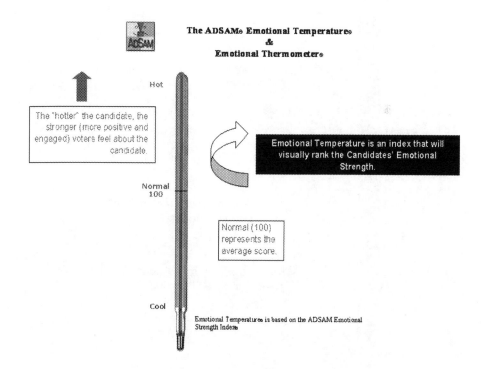

Image 2: Emotional Temperature

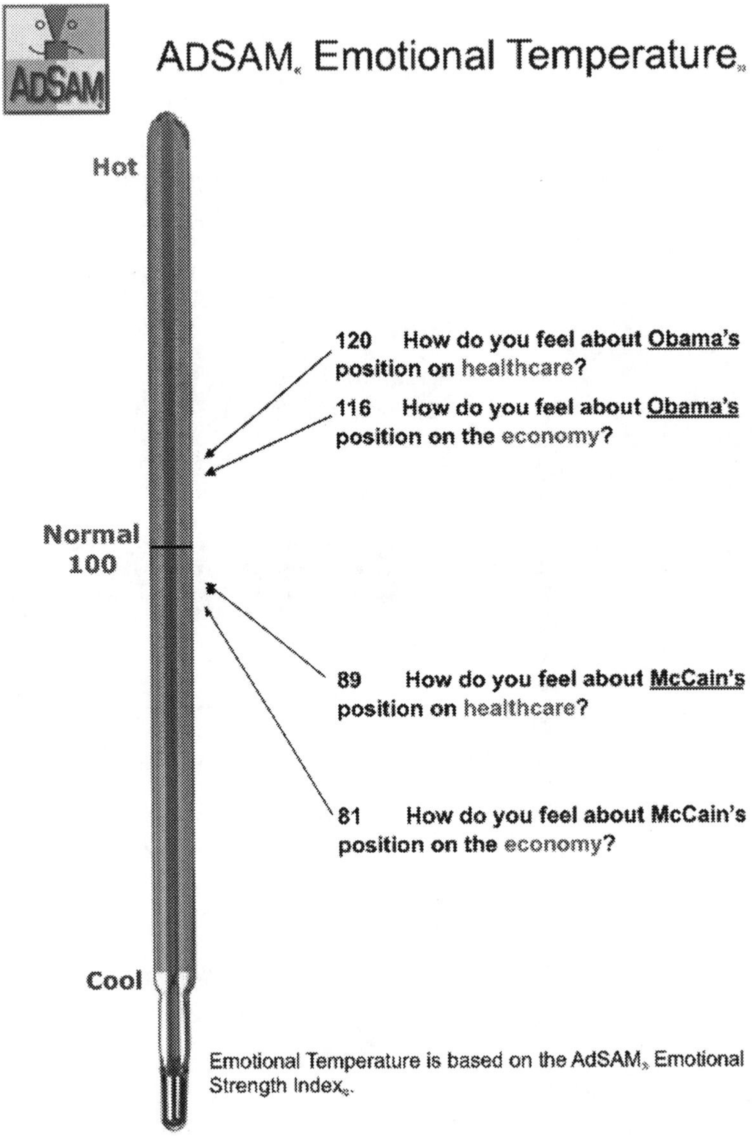

ADSAM. Emotional Temperature.

Hot

120   How do you feel about <u>Obama's</u> position on healthcare?

116   How do you feel about <u>Obama's</u> position on the economy?

Normal 100

89   How do you feel about <u>McCain's</u> position on healthcare?

81   How do you feel about McCain's position on the economy?

Cool

Emotional Temperature is based on the AdSAM. Emotional Strength Index.

Image 3: Total Sample for Barack Obama and John McCain

The ADSAM® measure is based on the three-dimensional PAD theory of emotion which states that every emotion is a combination of three dimensions:

Pleasure—measures like/dislike or level of appeal

(The only true positive/negative dimension)

Arousal—measures the level of involvement or excitement

Dominance—measures the level of empowerment

- The two primary factors evaluated in the emotional response data are:

    - the nature of the feelings evoked—provides insight into emotional connectors, impact, needs, barriers and receptivity

    - the degree of homogeneity in the responses—provides insight into the strength of perception, need or barrier.

In summarise, as we may note all voters felt more confident in Obama's rather than in McCain's position on the most important issues—healthcare and the economy, during the Presidential campaign in the United States.

Economy: Obama leads McCain by 35 emotional strength points

Healthcare: Obama leads McCain by 31 emotional strength points

'Instant of intrusion in to the everyday. (. . .) It is what constantly demands to be explained and re-explained.'[121] was analysed already in this paper and is worthy of repetition. Obama's performance and the way he presented his new solutions for the crucial issues of the United States made people respond with a high level of excitement and involvement to it. However, did he really have such a strong and realistic vision of the healthcare and economic reforms?

---

[121] Ibid., pp.84.

'If there's a blue pill and a red pill, and the blue pill is half
the price of the red pill and works just as well, why not pay
half price for the thing that's going to make you well?—
President Obama'[122]

That was the way President Obama presented the essential and real
problem, one the American Nation is facing right now—healthcare.
If this is the Obama's vision on how to solve the crucial issues of his
country, we all must admit that 'his vision' during the election time
'woke up' only via the American nation's imagination.

7.2 Qualitative Studies in the Educational/Creative Drama

'Prior qualitative studies have suggested that educational
drama creates real enthusiasm among participants and
that participants believe that it is a very effective learning
tool.'[123]

(Learning—understood as the 'cognitive process through which
people acquire and store knowledge, attitudes, or skills and change
their behaviour owning to an educational experience. The change in
behaviour may be related to knowledge, attitudes, believes, values,
skills, or performance')[124]

Pearce and Jackson (2006) Qualitative Research,

---

[122] Freddoso, D. Take the red pill, Mr. President. *Washington examiner*,
07/23/09, 6:56 AM EDT. [Internet] Available from: <http://www.
washingtonexaminer.com/opinion/blogs/beltway-confidential/Take-the-
red-pill-Mr-President-51473502.html>, [Accessed 29 August 2009].

[123] Ibid., pp.1.

[124] Holli, B.B., Calabrese, R.J., O'Sullivan, M.J. (2003) *Communication
and education skills for dietetics professionals.* XYZ editeur/XYZ
Publishing, pp.233.

The Concrete Example of Educational Drama in Marketing.[125]

In 2006, an Australian university, instigated research amongst its final year undergraduate marketing class students. The dramatic story used during the drama's process was 'The Poor', an Australian rock band on their way to the American market. However, it was only a hypothetical example, but still a very realistic business proposition. Students were supposed to fit into different characters: radio station executives from Sydney, record producers, Sony music executives, rock journalists, a rock historian, an industry writer/commentator, American radio disc jockeys, American television executives (one from MTV), marketing consultants, and tour promoters active in the American Market. The lecturer was playing the role of the meeting chair. He was the one who was greeting everyone and also was 'playing' some rock music supposedly by 'the Poor'.

The aim of that meeting was to promote 'The Poor' in America, but there was one more purpose—Austrade, the Australian marketing organisation wanted to make a better choice, between using the band to start off a 'Heavy Metal Down-Under' promotion in America, or a 'genre-neutral Australian cultural' one.

As the results showed, that vigorous improvised drama lasted for about one hour. It was an example of the 'Meeting' convention which is so crucial in educational/creative drama. The meeting is the core element of the drama. Furthermore, Pearce and Jackson (2006) reported that students who were taking part in this kind of drama, showed a high level of motivation and a strong sense of realism. Additionally, the students found it a very valuable source of getting to know, different, sometimes unexpected perspectives represented by others who experienced this kind of drama.

---

[125] Ibid., pp.3.

Code	Illustrative remarks
Communication	C1 "One of the main attributes which I have gained from this unit is confidence not only in my presentation skill but communication skill." C2 "It has increased my confidence in my drama ability and not be embarrassed to speak in front of people." C3 "I really enjoyed class. I had 100% attendance which is a reflection of the way I feel towards this class. It has built my confidence and helped me to be a better presenter."
Learning	L1 "Learning through drama brings knowledge to life." L2 "It is much more engaging and interesting than 'normal' teaching methods. I think it's a unit where you don't realise how much you learn immediately." L3 "I liked the class and I did not realise how much I had learned until I completed my diary." L4 "Reflecting on drama also has given me a deeper and meaningful learning experience as the relationship with theoretical models has time to evolve in the mind and draw innovative analysis on marketing material."
Social	S1 "I was fortunate to be part of a great class, the dynamics of this class further helped my learning and made the experience that much better." S2 "Not only has educational drama allowed me to improve my people skills, my confidence and knowledge, it's been fun, enjoyable and I would recommend everyone to do it."
Real	R1 "It is very useful in demonstrating practical marketing concepts in the real world." R2 "Simulation of real life situations; therefore good experience to be applied in the workplace and the real world of marketing." R3 "Educational drama brought a practical element to theories and models previously taught as well as current marketing issues. This greatly aids in the understanding and application of this theory."

Image 4: The Illustrative Remarks Made by the Participants of the Pearce and Jackson's (2006) Qualitative Research in Educational/Creative Drama.[126]

Comments, which were made by the students after the drama, were coded to the Communication and Social Categories. Logically, we may assume that dramatic improvisation helped them in communication and socialisation. Moreover, what seams to be very interesting, is the fact that some students' remarks were coded under the Real Category. Thus, we are able to address the question—how can dramatic improvisation bring a reality into existence? As we can note, thanks to Pearce and Jackson (2006) research and via the students' perception, it can.

---

[126] The Illustrative Remarks Made by the Participants of the Pearce and Jackson's (2006) Qualitative Research in Educational/Creative Drama. [Online Image]. Available from: <http://www. new1.heacademy.ac.uk/ assets/bmaf/documents/publications/IJME/accepted_for_publication/ IJME237.pdf>, [Accessed 29 August 2009].

Variable	Mean	Standard deviation
Communication skills		
"Doing educational drama has helped me develop my presentational skills" (Presentation)	3.6	0.643
"Doing educational drama has helped me develop my skill in writing" (Writing)	2.6	0.819
Learning		
"Educational drama helps me understand theoretical concepts" (Theory)	3.3	0.569
"Educational drama is helpful in understanding complex problems" (Understanding)	3.1	0.640
"I learn a lot when educational drama is used" (Learning method)	3.2	0.844
Social skills		
"Doing educational drama gives me the confidence to express opinions" (Confidence)	3.3	0.740
"Doing educational drama has helped me develop my team-working skills" (Team work)	3.6	0.644
Real world		
"Educational drama illustrates how business/marketing works in the real world" (Real)	3.5	0.577
"Educational drama helps me understand how business decisions are made" (Decisions)	3.2	0.612

Student perceptions of learning through educational drama

Note: Variables measured using a 4-point scale: 1= strongly disagree, 4 = strongly agree, midpoint = 2.5

Image 5; The Illustrative Quantitative Results of Remarks Made by the Participants of the Pearce and Jackson's (2006) Qualitative Research in Educational/Creative Drama.[127]

In addition to the results stated above, in all cases, students strongly agreed that educational/creative drama was of benefit in developing presentation, learning and social skills, bringing in the real word even to fictional settings. Furthermore, we can support this paper, along with the research Pearce and Jackson (2006), by the following:

Previously stated, and explained is how the American Nation's political drama took place in the United States during the Presidential Election with Obama in the role of leader and conductor of this process as creative/educational (chapter 4.7 of this paper). His drama

---

[127] The Illustrative Quantitative Results of Remarks Made by the Participants of the Pearce and Jackson's (2006) Qualitative Research in Educational/Creative Drama.[Online Image]. Available from: <http://www-new1.heacademy.ac.uk/assets/bmaf/documents/publications/IJME/accepted_for_publication/IJME237.pdf>, [Accessed 29 August 2009].

was the one that brought into being the elements of the fictional world, the new world which the American Nation is supposed to make an actual (chapter 4.3 of this paper). Moreover, the Obama's performance created a 'high level of involvement and excitement' (chapter 8.1 of this paper). Thus, following the Pearce and Jackson (2006) research, we may be able to justify, as to how the American drama process brought into existence the strong communication and socialisation skills between the American Nation as well as, what is crucial for the reasons of this paper, reality. The American Nation perceived that, which was created and performed—even if supported by fictional settings—could be their reality.

7.3 Creative Imagination

'Imagination articulate energizes and metamorphoses reality into dreams and dreams into reality, and by whose logic we turn away from the fetters of easy imitation to soar in the regions of liberty. (Young, 1759).'[128]

Can we awaken people's creative imagination, via the power of the spoken word, such as in Barack Obama's oratory? Eccles suggested that, by the relationship between images: one image is evocative of the other and when they are merged into one language-verbal creation, a pleasing combination of elements appears. Thus, it brings in to being a transcendent experience in others. Moreover, 'to this kind of imagery (we may) add an entirely different order of image-making which provides the illumination that gives a new insight or understanding and relative to science it may take the form of a new hypothesis.'[129] We may assume that our imagination may be roused, not only by seeing images, but also via the auditory senses.

---

[128] Khatena. J. (1977) Creative Imagination and What We Can Do to Stimulate it. *Gifted Child Quarterly.* 21 (84), pp.83-97.

[129] Khatena, J. (1975) Creative Imagination Imagery and Analogy. *Gifted Child Quarterly,* 19 (149)

'It's time to turn the page on education—to move past the slow decay of indifference'[130]

To express our thoughts, feelings and the way that we view our surroundings we use words. We find it difficult to describe verbally many of our experiences. Thus, we are looking for solutions, expressions that will bring to life the images, which we have in minds. We are trying to find some analogy that will make the 'strange' more describable. In addition, this process leads us to the creation of analogies, the so called 'synthetic approach to creative problem solving' (Gordon, 1961). There are four kinds of analogy: personal, direct, fantasy and symbolic. For the reason of this paper we need to focus on the fantasy and personal analogy.

1. The Fantasy Analogy.[131]

In this kind of analogy the object or subject being compared with the other must at least be imaginary. As for example: Pandora's Box, Angels, and the Medusa, Paradise. In addition, we may be able to ad one more—Dreams. Thus, with America we may create the structure called—the fantasy analogy—the American Dream (chapter 4.6 of this paper)—which so regularly appears in Obama's speeches. "I still have a dream. It is a dream deeply rooted in the American dream."[132]

---

[130] Ibid.,

[131] Ibid., pp.90.

[132] Ibid.,(King, M.L, *I Have a Dream Speech*)

2. The Personal Analogy; Dr. Martin Luther King and Barack Obama.[133]

(. . .) So, did Obama, during the Presidential Elections in the United States, manage to create a brand new idea of his 'vision'? Assuming that the tool which he used was the alienation effect, and as this paper was trying to explain (chapter 3.1, 6.1, 6.2 of this paper) Obama did employ this effect during his performance. It seems to be more then obvious that 'his' vision was created by the American Nation's creative imagination.

---

[133] Ibid., pp.90.

7.3.1 The Alienation Effect in Modern Advertisement.

Image 6: Mercedes-Benz ad[134]

'Contemporary ad designers (as well as visual artists, musicians, and actors) have appropriated this technique to highlight the machinery of their production for the reader, establishing a tacit acknowledgement that They know We know we are being manipulated by the visual rhetoric, and letting readers be part of the inside joke. However, in doing so, they create another layer of manipulation and meaning and effectively undermine the reader's potential for activism and understanding the real nature of the rhetoric.'[135]

---

[134] Mercedes-Benz ad. Duecom, Porto Alegre, Brazil, advertising agency. Juliano Weide, creative director.João Ricardo Mello and Duda Couto, copywriters. Published Dec. 2008. *Ads of the World*.
26 Jan. 09 [Online image] Available from: <http://adsoftheworld.com/media/print/mercedesbenz_emptyfull)>, [Accessed 29 August 2009].

[135] Koller, L., The machinery of Design: Playing with Brecht, the Surrealists, on Proactive Images. *Design. Principles & Practices: An International Journal*, 3(3), pp.167. [Internet] Available from: <http://www.cosmicscribbler.com/files/Machineryofdesign.pdf>, [Accessed 29 August 2009].

This Brazilian ad for Mercedes-Benz published in December 2008, is representative of Brecht's alienation effect the letter E being an explicit, typographic acknowledgement that the mode of production spits out a printed page and no amount of vivid imagery of throbbing diesel engines propelling shiny red cars over the Pacific Highway will compensate for the magnitude of real gravel, metal, and pistons. The E/F visual makes the car the difference between being empty and being full. The aim ad meant to influence the reader, but actually the reader can take control and affect her own reality by purchasing the car incorporated into the E. While the E may act as an alienation effect point out the "theatre" in situ, to reveal the myths surrounding the "American dream = car," the ad speaks more of maintaining the fourth wall, rather than disrupting it. Here, theatre is the hyper-reality of the distended symbol. Autos themselves are distensions of reality—rarely do we mediate our experiences with them through their use and place, but rather through their act as conspicuous consumption and symbolism of the bourgeoisie. Since autos are a mediating figure between people's social relations, the E, distends that one step further: fuel efficiency is itself now a new angle to the American dream. We can meet as people—no mediation between us; or we meet through a distension of our vehicles. They are a facade of what we wish ourselves to be, and so I/my car meets your car/then you. Thus, we experience distension from reality, which sharpens the hyper-reality of a symbol, making the symbol become its own referent. If we can say that art is art when it breaches the fourth wall, reduces or exposes hyper-reality, and lessens levels of distension, then the ad works in both ways: maintaining the fourth wall and blasting through the fourth wall, building hyper-reality and lessening hyper-reality, forming more distension and lessening distensions.

8. Why Did Barack Obama Succeed, when Jesse Jackson, John McCain and Hilary Clinton—failed?

'I am in, and I am to win'[136] (Hillary Rodham Clinton)

'You must not surrender! You may or may not get there but just know that you're qualified! And you hold on, and hold out! We must never surrender!! America will get better and better.'[137] (Jesse Jackson)

'I fight for Americans. I fight for you.'[138] (John McCain)

'But this campaign that we're running has to be about your hopes, and your dreams, and what you will do.'[139]

(Barack Obama)

---

[136] Ibid., (Clinton, H.R., *Announcement to Run for U.S. President*, Jan. 20, 2007)

[137] Jackson, J. Speech. 1988 Democratic National Convention Address, delivered 19 July 1988, Omni Coliseum, Atlanta GA. [Internet] Available from: <C:\Documents and Settings\r01jeb8\Desktop\American Rhetoric Jesse Jackson—1988 Democratic National Convention Address.htm>, [Accessed 29 August 2009].

[138] Harnden, T. Text of John McCain's Republican convention speech in St Paul. *The Daily Telegraph*, (September 5th, 2008). [Internet] Available from: <http://blogs.telegraph.co.uk/news>, [Accessed 29 August 2009].

[139] Ibid., (Obama, B. *Turn the page speech*)

For the reasons of this paper, it seems to be more than crucial to try to answer the question of why Barack Obama won the election and why Jesse Jackson, John McCain or Hillary Clinton did not make it? To extrapolate further, the Obama charismatic leadership was a drama process, (chapter 3.2,4,5 of this paper). Furthermore, each drama process' aim is to transform individually, each of its participants. Thus, each charismatic leadership leads its participants, via the alienation effect (chapter 3.1 & 6 of this paper) in the manner of awakening their own dreams and hopes and via this kind of mobilisation to the nation's further actions. Essentially, in this scenario, the leader is a 'shepherd', and the nation is a 'flock' (Foucault),[140] (chapter 3.3 of this paper).

The aim of the charismatic leadership is the process of leading or conducting the nation towards their own personal direction but united in terms of their tradition and culture, (chapter 3.4, 4.6 of this paper). In addition, this is the primary aim of the alienation effect, which from one perspective is preventing the nation from 'stepping into the leader's shoes', as well as demanding the answers from the leader. The other perspective leads the whole nation to look for the answers by themselves. Moreover, charismatic leadership is not the process of the personal leader's fight, or the fight of the whole nation as Jesse Jackson, Hillary Rodham Clinton or McCain suggested. The charismatic leadership is:

> 'art of conducting, directing, leading, guiding, handling, manipulating human beings, an art of pursuing them (. . .) collectively and individually throughout their life and at each moment of their existence'[141]

---

[140]   Prozorov, S. (2007) *Foucault, freedom and sovereignty.* Ashgate Publishing, Ltd, pp.105.

[141]   Siemens, H.W., Roodt V. (2008). *Nietzsche, Power and Politics: Rethinking Nietzsche's Legacy for Political Thought.* Walter de Gruyter, pp.722.

Obama's leadership was the only one which successfully used Foucault's technology of individualisation, and which in its essence led to the effect as 'charisma'. The Foucault's technology of individualisation (chapter 3.3 of this paper) may be in its roots, compared with the Brecht's alienation effect: the tool, in both cases (theatrical as well as political performance) was able to reach each individual and their inner truth; separate and isolate individual subjects from the whole nation. Moreover, through the Foucault's technique of confession (chapter 3.3 of this paper) the leader is able to unite and direct each of them in one traditional/cultural direction. The leader of charismatic relation as Obama used the technique of confession—his life story (chapter 4.7, 4.8 of this paper)—that became an "alluring puzzle":

> 'when we use our imagination are in the first place stirred by some alluring puzzle which calls for a solution, and in the second place enabled by our own creations in the mind to see much that was before dark or unintelligible. (Harold Rugg, 1963)'[142]

This led to the next, the technique of individualisation/alienation, which led each individual from the American Nation to the creation of his/her personal vision, the vision of their future life. The vision of their future life may become real and actual if followed, not only by the leader's actions, but by the American Nation itself.

The pastoral power (chapter 3.3 of this paper) is based on the technology of individualisation/alienation—different dynamics. The technique of confession is a tool of the technology of individualisation. The leader, (one individual from the nation) and the rest of the nation, have their roots in tradition and culture. Thus, charisma is not a 'top to toe' process, or its reversal. The leadership charisma is the process of the relationship within the whole nation based on different dynamics (which have been initialised via drama

---

[142] Ibid., pp.149.

process in forms of different ideas, dreams, plans—created by each individual from the nation by their imagination) with the leader as a conductor/shepherd (as well as being one of the nation) The leader only gives the pretext, the so called story (his personal 'confession') to start the action as the charismatic visionary leadership, co-created with the rest of the nation.

1.

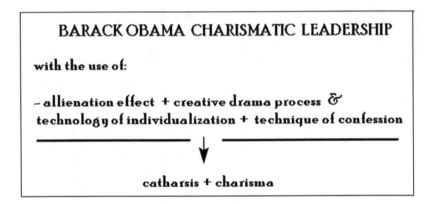

1a.

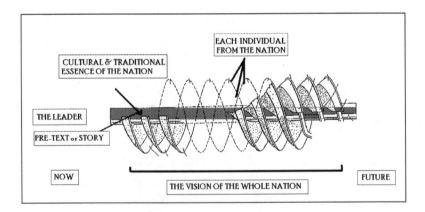

Images 1&1a: Charismatic Visionary Leadership.

2.

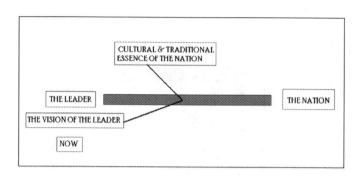

2a.

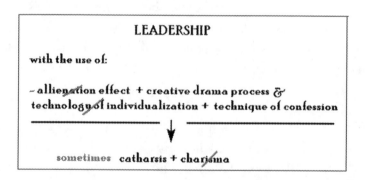

2b.

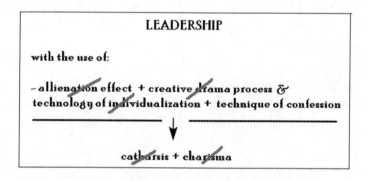

**Images 2&2a&2b: Cathartic Leadership
and the Ordinary Leadership**

9. Conclusion

A few months ago, somebody gave me a book on 'BullShit' (Prof. H. Frankfurt, Princeton University)[143]. This book was a great inspiration for this work. I also learned that politics is never about finding the answers; it is always about finding the questions. Our all life is dedicated to discovery, challenge and the pushing of ourselves to the edge of possibilities of the mind. From this we gain knowledge but also question the present, the past and all those Greats, who day by day, again and again, give us the inspiration and the ideas for our own 'discoveries'.

Thoughts, and ways of thinking, give us our substance and personal essence, which make us so individualistic but, conversely, allow as to closely relate to each other. Our 'here and now', our reality or actuality is deeply rooted in our beliefs, hopes and plans for the future. That is the reason why it is never about 'bullshit', but is always about Hoping, Dreaming and our Imagination, as well as about the way how we negotiate and renegotiate our thoughts with those who create with us the 'here and now'.

This paper and future research are dedicated to the political world, which is increasingly becoming virtual, in a visionary leadership, created by each of us, in our own personal way.

---

[143] Frankfurt, H. *BullShit*. Princeton University. [Internet] Available from: <http://www.gwinnettdailyonline.com/articleB5BD6D4417AF444D BD8F9770AA729B26.asp>, [Accessed 29 August 2009].

Bibliography

Alexander, J. C. (ed.) (Ed.). (1989) Durkheim Ian sociology: Cultural studies. Berkeley: University of California press.

Aristotle, (2004) Poetics. Kessinger Publishing Co.

Baumeister, R. F., Leary, M. R. (1995) The need to belong: Desire for interpersonal attachments as a fundamental human motivation. Psychological Bulletin 117, pp.497-529.

Bendix, R. (1977) Max Weber: An intellectual portrait. London: Methuen.

Bendix, R. (19860 Reflections on charismatic leadership. R. Glassman & R. Swatos (eds.). Charisma, history and social structure, pp. 17-25. New York: greenwood press.

Bennis, W., Nanus, B. (1986) Leaders. New York: Harper perennial, Harper Collins publishers.

Bensman, J., Givant, M. (1986) Charisma and modernity. In R. Glassman & R. Swatos (eds.). Charisma, history and social structure, pp. 52-56. New York: greenwood press.

Bligh, M.C., Kohles J. C. (2009) The enduring allure of charisma: How Barack Obama won the historic 2008 presidential election. The Leadership Quarterly, Volume 20, Issue 3, June, p. 483-492.

Brecht, B., Bentley E., (1961) On Chinese Acting. The Tulane Drama Review, 6(1) September, the MIT Press, pp.130-136.

Brecht, B., Willett, J. (1964) Brecht on theatre: the development of an aesthetic. Hill and Wang.

Bunge, M.A. (1977) Ontology. Volume 1, Springer.

Burke, K. (1925) Psychology and form. The Dial.

Carr, B. (1996) Morals and society in Asian Society. Routledge.

Chinoy, E. (1967) Society: an introduction to sociology. Random House.

Clark, E.M., Brock, T.C., Stewart, B.D. (1994) Attention, attitude, and affect in response to advertising. Lawrence Erlbaum Associates.

Clifford, M. (2001) Political genealogy after Foucault: savage identities. Routledge.

Cohn, R. (1982) New American Dramatists: 1960-1080. New York: The MacMillan Press Ltd, pp.28-29.

Conger, J.A. (1989) The charismatic leader. Behind the mystique of exceptional leadership. San Francisco: Jossey-Bass.

Conger, J.A., Kanungo, Charismatic leadership: The elusive factor in organizational effectiveness. San Francisco: Jossey-Bass, pp.213-236.

Conger, J.A., Kanungo, R.N. (1987) Towards a behavioural theory of charismatic leadership in organizational settings. Academy of Management, Review 12 (4), pp.637-647.

Courtney, R. (1990) Drama and Intelligence: A Cognitive Theory. Montreal, McGill-Queen's University Press.

Cullen, J. (2004) The American dream: a short history of an idea that shaped a nation. Oxford University Press.

Davy, K. (1978) Richard Foreman's Ontological-Hysteric Theatre: The Influence of Gertrude Stein. Twentieth Century Literature, 24 (1) Spring.

Davis, D. (1997) Interactive research in drama in education, Trentham Books, 1997.

Debord G., Nicholson-Smith, D. (1994) The Society of the Spectacle, Published by Zone Books.

Drain, R., (1995) Twentieth Century Theatre: A Sourcebook, Routledge.

During, S. (2004) Foucault and Literature: Towards a Genealogy of Writing. Routledge.

Dyer, R. (1991) Charisma. Stardom: Industry of desire, ed. C. Gledhill.

Eisenstadt, S. (1968) Max Weber on charisma and institution building. Chicago: University of Chicago press.

Fawcett, E.D. (1939) Oberland dialogues. Macmillan and Co., Limited.

Ferri, A.J. (2007) Willing suspension of disbelief: poetic faith in film. Lexington Books, pp.103.

Elam, K. (1980) The semiotics of theatre and drama. Methuen Publishing Ltd.

Foucault, M. (2006) History of Madness, Translated by Jean Khalfa, Jonathan Murphy, Routledge.

Foucault, M. (2007) The Archaeology of Knowledge: Includes the Discourse on Language, Published by Pantheon Books, Original from the University of Michigan.

Foucault, M. (1999) Religion and culture: Michel Foucault, edited by Jeremy R. Carrette.

Foucault, M. (1998) The History of Sexuality Vol. 1: The Will to Knowledge. London: Penguin.

Foucault, M. (1992) The History of Sexuality Vol. 2: The Use of Pleasure. London: Penguin.

Foucault, M. (1990) The History of Sexuality Vol. 3: The Care of Self. London: Penguin.

Foucault, M., Burchell, G., Gordon, C., Miller, P. (1991) The Foucault effect: studies in governmentality: with two lectures by and an interview with Michel Foucault. University of Chicago Press.

Freud. S. (1922) Group psychology and the analysis of the ego. London: International psycho-analytic al press. Friedland, W. 1964 for a sociological concept of charisma. Social forces, 43, pp.18-26.

Furlong, E.J., (2004) Imagination. Volume 7 of Muirhead library of philosophy. Routledge.

Gardner, William L., Avolio, B. J. (1998) The charismatic relationship: A dramaturgical perspective. Academy of management review, 23, pp. 32-58.

Gassner, J. (1954) Dramatic and Detachment: A View of Brecht's Style of Theatre. The Theatre in Our Times: A Survey of the

Men, Materials and Movements in the Modern Theatre. New York: Crown Publishers, p.82-99.

Glassman, R. (1986) Charisma and social structure—the success or failure of charismatic leadership. In R. Glassman and R. Swatos (Eds) Charisma, history and social structure, pp. 179-205. New York greenwood pres.

Goffman, E. (1959) The presentation of self in everyday life, Volume 174 of Doubleday anchor books Anchor books, Issue 2 of University of Edinburgh. Social Services Research Centre. Monograph. Doubleday.

Gray, R.D. (1976) Brecht the Dramatist. New York: Cambridge University Press.

Gutting, G. (1944) The Cambridge companion to Foucault. Cambridge University Press.

Heathcote, D. (1977). Drama as challenge. In J. Hodgson (Ed.).The uses of drama: Acting as a social and educational force. London: Eyre Methuen.

Hindess, B. (1996) Discourses of Power: from Hobbes to Foucault. Wiley-Blackwell.

Harland, R. (1987) Superstructuralism: The Philosophy of Structuralism and Post-structuralism, Published by Routledge.

Hobbes, T. (2002) Leviathan, translated by W.E. Krul, Uitgeverij Boom.

Holli, B.B., Calabrese, R.J., O'Sullivan, M.J. (2003) Communication and education skills for dietetics professionals. XYZ editeur/XYZ Publishing.

Horton, D., Wohl, R. (1956) Mass communication and Para social interaction: Observation on intimacy at a distance. Psychiatry 19(3), pp.188-211.

House, R. J., Baetz, M. (1979) Leadership: Some empirical generalizations and new research directions, Research in organizational behaviour, 1, pp.341-423. Greenwich, CT: JAI press.

House, R. J., Spangler, W. D., Woycke, J. (1991) Personality and charisma in the U.S. presidency: A psychological theory of leader effectiveness. Administrative science quarterly, 36, pp.364-396.

Jameson, F. (2000) Brecht and method. Verso, pp.84.

Kaufmann, H. (1973) Social psychology: the study of human interaction. Holt, Rinehart and Winston.

Khatena, J. (1975) Creative Imagination Imagery and Analogy. Gifted Child Quarterly, 19 (149).

Khatena. J. (1977) Creative Imagination and What We Can Do to Stimulate it. Gifted Child Quarterly. 21 (84).

Kirk, J.A. (2005) Martin Luther King Jr. Profiles in power. Pearson Education.

Lipp, W. (1985) Stigma and Charisma. Berlin: Dietrich Reimer.

Lindholm, C. (1990) Charisma. Cambridge MA.

Martin, C., Bial, H. (2000) Brecht Sourcebook. Routledge.

McDonald, M., Walton, J.M. (2007) The Cambridge companion to Greek and Roman theatre. Cambridge University Press.

McGuigan, J. (1996) Culture and the public sphere. Taylor & Francis.

McHoul, A., Grace, W. (1995) A Foucault primer: discourse, power and the subject. Routledge.

McTeague, J. H. (1994) Playwrights and Acting: Acting Methodologies for Brecht, Ionesco, Pinter, and Shepard. Westport: Greenwood Press.

Mumford, M. (2009) Bertolt Brecht.Taylor & Francis.

Prozorov, S. (2007) Foucault, freedom and sovereignty. Ashgate Publishing, Ltd.

Raphael, D.D. (2004) Hobbes: morals and politics. Routledge.

Rasche, A. (2007) The Paradoxical Foundation of Strategic Management. Springer.

Roose-Evans, J. (1984) Experimental theatre from Stanislavsky to Peter Brook, Routledge.

Rosenau, P.M. (1992) Post-modernism and the Social Sciences. Princeton: Princeton UP.

Rouse, J. (1984) Brecht and the Contradictory Actor, Theatre Journal, 36 (1) Mar., The Interpretive Actor, pp. 25-42.

Salaman, G., Storey, J., Billsberry J. (2005) Strategic human resource management: theory and practice. SAGE.

Sarup, M. (1988) An Introductory Guide to Post-structuralism and Postmodernism, Harvester Wheatsheaf.

Severin, W.J., Tankard, J.W. Jr. (1979) Communication Theories: Origins, Methods, Uses. New York: Hastings House.

Shank, T. (2002) Beyond the boundaries: American alternative theatre. University of Michigan Press.

Shils, E. (1965) Charisma. Order and status. In E. shills (ed.) Centre and periphery: Essays in macro sociology, pp. 256-257. Chicago: university of Chicago press.

Shils, E. (1968) The concentration and dispersion of charisma. in E. Shils (ed.), centre and periphery: Essays in macro sociology, pp. 405-421. Chicago: university of Chicago press.

Silverman, K. (1984) The Subject of Semiotics. New York: Oxford University Press.

Silverman, K., The threshold of the visible world, Routledge, 1996

Siemens, H.W., Roodt V. (2008). Nietzsche, Power and Politics: Rethinking Nietzsche's Legacy for Political Thought. Walter de Gruyter.

Smith, A.D. (1996) Culture, Community and Territory: The Politics of Ethnicity and Nationalism. Ethnicity and International Relations, 72 (3) July, Blackwell Publishing on behalf of the Royal Institute of International Affairs, pp. 445-458.

Stanislavsky, K. (1990) An Actor's Handbook: An Alphabetical Arrangement of Concise Statements on Aspects of Acting. London: Methuen.

Stanislavsky, K. (1988) An Actor Prepares. London: Methuen.

Stanislavsky, K. (1988) An Actor's Work: A Student's Diary.

Stanislavsky, K. (2008) Building a Character. New York: Theatre Arts Books, London: Routledge.

Stanislavsky, K. (1968) Creating a Role. London: Mentor, 1968.

Staudt, A., Weaver, W.G. (1997) Political science & feminisms, New York: Twayne Publishers.

Stauffer, R.M. (1927) The progress of drama, through the centuries. Macmillan.

Steele, R., Swinney S.V. (1982) Freud and Jung, conflict of interpretation. Law Book Co of Australasia.

Stevenson, K. (1995) The fourth wall and the third space. Centre for Playback Theatre.

Steyrer, J. (1998) Charisma and the Archetypes of Leadership. Organization Studies, Vol. 19, No. 5, p. 807-828.

Taylor, P. The drama classroom: action, reflection, transformation, Routledge, 2000.

Thomson, P., Sacks, G. (2006) The Cambridge companion to Brecht. Cambridge University Press.

Toye, N., Prendiville, F. (2000) Drama and Traditional Story for the Early Years, Routledge.

Truman.H.S., Hillman W., Mr. President: The First Publication from the Personal Diaries, Private Letters, Papers and Revealing Interviews of Harry S. Truman.

Wagner, B.J. (1999) Building moral communities through educational drama. Greenwood Publishing Group.

Weber, M. (1977) On Charisma and Institution Building. Chicago: Yale University Press.

Weissberg, R., (1975) Political Efficacy and Political, The Journal of Politics, 37 (20) May, pp.469-487.

Whyman, R. (2008) The Stanislavsky system of acting: legacy and influence in modern performance. Cambridge University Press.

Zaleznik, A. (1992) Managers and Leaders: Are They Different?, Harvard Business Review, March-April, pp. 126-135.

Internet Sources:

Clinton, H.R., Announcement to Run for U.S. President, Jan. 20, 2007. Available from: <http://www.msnbc.msn.com/id/16720167/>

Frankfurt, H., BullShit. Princeton University. Available from: http://www.gwinnettdailyonline.com/articleB5BD6 D4417AF444DBD8F9770AA729B26.asp

Freddoso, D. Take the red pill, Mr. President. Washington examiner, 07/23/09, 6:56 AM EDT. Available from: http://www. washingtonexaminer.com/opinion/blogs/beltway-confidential/ Take-the-red-pill-Mr-President-51473502.html

Harnden, T., Text of John McCain's Republican convention speech in St Paul. The Daily Telegraph, (September 5th, 2008). Available from: http://blogs.telegraph.co.uk/news

Jackson, J. Speech. 1988 Democratic National Convention Address, delivered 19 July 1988, Omni Coliseum, Atlanta GA. Available from: <C:\Documents and Settings\r01jeb8\Desktop\American

Rhetoric Jesse Jackson—1988 Democratic National Convention Address.htm>

King, M.L. I have a dream speech. August 28, 1963, Available from: http://www.presentationhelper.co.uk/martin_luther_king_speech. htm

King, M.L. Speech, Riverside Church, April 4, 1967. Available from: http://letterfromhere.blogspot.com/2009/01/perhaps-new-spirit-is-rising-among-us.html

Kiwonlee, B.A. (2001) The Dynamics of Richard Foreman's Theatre: Text and performance Available from: http://etd.lib. ttu.edu/theses/available/etd-09262008-31295017969758/unrestricted/31295017969758.pdf

Koller, L., The machinery of Design: Playing with Brecht, the Surrealists, on Proactive Images. Design. Principles & Practices: An International Journal, 3(3), pp.167. Available from: <http://www.cosmicscribbler.com/files/Machineryofdesign.pdf>

Lindholm, C. (2002) Charisma. Available from: http://www.bu.edu/uni/faculty/profiles/charisma.pdf

Malkin, B., Barack Obama has made Martin Luther King's dream a reality, Telegraph. 11:14AM GMT 05 Nov 2008. Available from: http://www.telegraph.co.uk/news/worldnews/

Miller, S., US elections 2008: Why Barack Obama epitomizes the American dream. Helium. Available from: <http://www.helium. com/items/1215419-us-elections-2008-why-barack-obama-epitomizes-the-american-dream>

Nagourney, A., The New York Post, Obama Elected President as Racial Barrier Falls, November 4, 2008. Available from: http://www.nytimes.com/2008/11/05/us/politics/05elect.html

SenseUs Emotional ResponsePolling. Available from: <http://senseus. net/file_download/27>

The election of Barack Obama, 5 November 2008. World Socialist Website.

Available from: <http://www.wsws.org/articles/2008/nov2008/pers-n05. shtml>

The Obama effect: Researchers cite President's role in reducing racism. Thursday, February 12, 2009—11:38, Psychology & Sociology. Available from: http://esciencenews.com/ articles/2009/02/12/the.obama.effect.researchers.cite.presidents. role.reducing.racism

The White House. [Internet] Available from: http://www.whitehouse. gov/administration/President_Obama/

Tomsky, M. Obama administration. Michael Tomasky's blog, Thursday 13 August 2009. Available from: http://www.guardian.co.uk/ commentisfree/michaeltomasky+world/obama-administration

Internet Sources—The Speeches of Barack Obama:

Acceptance speech, Wednesday 5 November 2008, Available from: www.guardian.co.uk

California Democratic National Convention speech, July 27, 2004. Available from: http://www.barackobama.com/2004/07/27/ keynote_address_at_the_2004_ de_1.php

Our Past, Future & Vision for America, February 10, 2007, Obama Presidential Announcement Springfield, Available from: http:// obamaspeeches.com

Turn the Page Speech, California Democratic National Convention, April 28, 2007. Available from: http://obamaspeeches.com/

Manassas, Prince William County, Virginia November 3, 2008, 10:30pm—Night Before the Election speech, Available from: http://obamaspeeches.com/